CULTIVATE

THE PROCESS OF LIVING FROM YOUR HEART

cultivate

cul·ti·vate \ˈkəl-tə-ˌvāt\

: to prepare and use for the raising of crops

: to loosen or break up the soil

: to foster the growth of

: to improve by labor, care, or study

: further, encourage

: to seek the society of

: make friends with

WELCOME

While planning our second volume of *Cultivate*, we chose to focus on the beauty of the Lord in winter seasons of life. We created this issue to champion the significance of our roots growing deep into His heart, and our branches resting from producing fruit. May your perspective of winter be altered by the stories you read and the moments you initiate with the Father, Son and Holy Spirit through the prompts in this book.

In these pages you will find recipes for spending time with the Lord and be prompted to journal His voice. Jesus says in John 10:27 ESV, "My sheep hear my voice, and I know them, and they follow me". As a child of God, you know His voice; you hear Him, and it is important that you record, savor and declare His thoughts over your life. By recording His thoughts, you will remember how deeply He loves you and who you truly are. Be courageous! It is in this process that our minds are transformed and we are able to live confidently as sons and daughters.

We encourage you to center your heart in this simple truth: God is a loving Father, ready and eager to speak to you. It is our hope that through these pages, you will be inspired to draw close to Him, that you will come into a better understanding of His nature and that you will dare to believe that you are who He says you are.

01

RECIPES & PROMPTS

recipe$_2$: a way of doing something that will produce a particular result
: a set of instructions for making something from various ingredients

prompt$_3$: to move to action
: incite
: to assist by suggesting or saying the next words of something forgotten or imperfectly learned

02

DEFINING MOMENTS & STORIES

defining moment : a point at which the essential nature or character
of a person, group, etc., is revealed or identified[4]
: a specific moment in time when God's nature
is identified

story : a narration of the events in the life of a person[5]
: one's testimony of truth

03

CREATIVE WRITINGS & POEMS

creative writing : composition intended to engage the imagination
and inspire creativity, emotion and truth

poem$_6$: composition that is characterized by great
beauty of language or expression

THE CLARITY WINTER BRINGS

WRITTEN BY MELISSA HELSER
PHOTOGRAPHY BY JONATHAN HELSER

I have come to a place in my life of realizing that every season, whether easy or difficult, has some deep truth in it if I have ears that can hear and a heart that can be still. Sometimes reflecting back feels impossible, but hindsight can restore true vision to see what was really there. So many times what was really there was a Bethlehem moment, ready to birth the truth of the Mighty One in my heart. This is my hindsight.

It was March of 2012, and I was in the thick of recovering from a very intense foot surgery. My toes, misshaped by a disease I have, had been curled to a point of impossibility. Impossible to wear shoes. Impossible to run and play with my kids. Impossible to get through a day without extreme pain. Impossible to feel beautiful barefoot. The impossibility of it all led me to a surgery that opened a door to some of the hardest three months of my life. I have had seasons of hardship. Having a chronic disease from the age of seventeen—walking through daily pain for seventeen years—has had its mountains high and valleys low, but nothing prepared me for the emotional heaviness that would fall. The doctors said it would be simple, a quick recovery. But seven toes broken, ten incisions and over fifty stitches was not simple and the recovery was not quick. The pain was unbearable and the heaviness so thick that I wondered if I would ever come out of it. I wondered if I would ever walk again. Had I made the worst mistake by doing this surgery? The days turned into weeks and the weeks into months, and my heart would sink and rise in and out of heartache. Lying in bed for weeks, feet in surgery shoes, only getting around on a walker like an old woman, took a toll on my heart like nothing ever had. You see, I have been sick a long time, but I have always faced life with an *I-will-not-waste-a-day* mentality. Pushing through the chronic pain to achieve a level of normality to keep me sane. Pushing through the lies and believing in the true goodness of God. Believing that His faithfulness was not and is not dependent on my circumstances but on His nature. His kindness has been my compass, guiding me through waters of uncertainty. His kindness has kept me safe when everything around me wasn't. But in this season, He seemed quiet and still when I needed Him to be loud and boisterous, filling my bedroom and heart with crazy joy. People would say, "You have all this time to sit, what is God teaching you?"

What is God teaching me? Does a father break his child's legs to teach him a lesson? I would cry out to the Father, "Did you allow this all to happen to get me still enough to teach me a lesson? You could have just told me." I would rant and rave and unravel my pain; and still in it all—silence.

Then one day, sitting on my back porch, bundled up from the chilling March air, I felt the presence of Jesus in such a real and tangible way. And finally He spoke, and the conversation went like this:

"Melissa, I am not sitting across from you cramming truth down your throat because you are still and cannot go anywhere. I am not taking advantage of this time to teach you a lesson. I am sitting next to you, holding your hand, crying with you and inviting you into a season of stillness, reflection and beauty. Beautiful Melissa, look into the woods. What do you see?"

I responded, "It is winter. I see the forest. Hundreds of trees. Trees that look dead. Barren."

He replied, "Yes, but don't you love how far you can see? Don't you love the clarity that winter brings?"

Immediately clarity came into my mind and heart. The fog lifted and the arms of a friend, my truest and most beautiful Friend, wrapped around me like the thickest, warmest blanket. Immediately I found myself understood. There I was in the middle of my winter—winter of the soul and winter of my world. There I was full of His presence, full of His beauty, full of His friendship. The clarity was Him—His comfort, His tenderness, His ability to reach into my sorrow and be present. The dark night of my thoughts submitted to the bright light of Jesus. He spoke again.

"If you walked into the woods and began to scream and cry and shout to the tallest oak and the mighty maple, 'Don't worry; don't be afraid. You will bloom again one day! Don't be disheartened— you will one day be covered with your brilliant leaves; spring will come,' they would lean down into your humanity and speak with wisdom so deep it would rattle your soul. They would say, 'Small person, we are not afraid. We are at rest. We are not anxious. We know that in the chill of the winter, we dig our roots deep into the earth. We are not dead and barren as you think. We are alive and living and growing. We know that even in seasons of stillness we grow, sometimes more than in seasons of fruitfulness.' Melissa, take a deep breath. You have been given the gift of a moment of stillness. I am not trying to teach you anything; I am wooing you into a gift. I am sending you an invitation, one that will change you forever. I sit next to you, holding your hand and whispering truth into your heart. This winter is your deepening. This winter is your gift."

I sat with tears of regret running down my face—regret that I had felt so abandoned by Him. I was looking for Him across from me, and the whole time He was next to me. I breathed Him in so deeply and the love of the Father filled my lungs. "I remain confident of this: I will see the goodness of the Lord in the land of the living" (Psalm 27:13, NIV). That day, the gift was seeing that I was in the midst of "the land of the living"—living things that seemed dead but were as alive as they had ever been. I saw, in that moment, my own bareness and the fragility of my perspective. I had misinterpreted the intent of the season. I had misinterpreted the intent of the Father. The gift was the restoration of my understanding of the nature of Jesus. The gift was Jesus not giving me what I thought I wanted, but healing my ability to understand Him. Healing my trust in Him. Healing my thoughts. Isn't that as much of a miracle as the healing of our bodies? To be made new in our minds. To think again and be made new in our perceptions. What I perceive now since that Bethlehem porch moment is that He is always present; sometimes I just need to look around. Sometimes I need to look again.

The winter has changed for me. Now, I get excited about seasons of stillness—seasons that feel quiet and almost unfruitful to the natural eye. I breathe deeper than I used to. The forest has changed for me; I love it as much in the middle of bareness as I do in the fullness of covering. I walk more in the winter than I do in the summer, and there, a mighty voice echoes into my heart: "Don't be afraid. Don't be anxious. You are more alive than you could ever imagine."

COLLECTIONS

The first time the Holy Spirit unwrapped the story of collecting in Joshua, I was deeply impacted. I could see how God understood humanity from the beginning and loved it deeply before Jesus came to the earth. Taken back by the humility of God as He helped the Israelites in a such a practical way, I said to the Holy Spirit, "I want to collect. I want to remember. Will you show me your love in a practical way?" As those words left my lips, I knew that God was grinning. A sudden thought came into my mind; it filled me with joy, and I knew it was the Holy Spirit: "What do you love, Justina?" I smiled and replied, "Feathers."

I was seventeen and in the middle of searching for myself and for God. I knew that He wanted to encounter me. I knew I wanted to encounter Him.

"and [Joshua] said to them, "Go over before the ark of the Lord your god into the middle of the Jordan. Each of you is to take up a stone on his shoulder, according to the number of the tribes of the Israelites, to serve as a sign among you. In the future, when your children ask you, 'What do these stones mean?' tell them that the flow of the Jordan was cut off before the ark of the covenant of the Lord...These stones are to be a memorial to the people of Israel forever."
Joshua 4:5-7, NIV

A lot shifted for me after that conversation. I found that some of my friendships began to change, and I encountered a loneliness that was unfamiliar. The silly drama of life, while nothing too severe, was painful enough for me to begin pulling away from people. I remember going on a walk when it was chilly outside, feeling sad and wondering why things turned out the way they did. I asked God, "Why does it have to be like this?" I paused, and I heard no answer. My heart sank, and I kept walking, looking at my feet. "Of course there is no answer. God doesn't care," I whispered under my breath. "He doesn't—" my grumbling was cut off because lying on the pavement right in front of me was a long feather. I picked it up. Immediately, I felt peace come over me. I remembered the conversation I had with the Holy Spirit, but the most important part was that He had remembered the conversation. This scenario happened countless times for three years. I would ask God a question, and His answer was never an explanation; it was a feather: the representation that God knew me, He knew what I liked, He knew what I needed. I gathered and collected, and I kept every one of those answers. Those three years were very important. I developed a close relationship with God and was changed forever. He pursued me through something insignificant to many but so important to me. God humbled Himself to my level and won my heart.

Nine years later, I look back on that time and smile. I remember how God changed my life. He walked through that one small door in my heart that I opened for Him at seventeen, and He walks through that same door everyday. He still finds me, and I still find Him.

Prompt: Pray this prayer: "Father, I thank you for pursuing me every day. I ask for a revelation of how much you really love me. I repent for making assumptions about your nature based on my circumstance. I confess that you are a good Father who cares deeply for me. I want to be friends with you, Holy Spirit, every day looking for evidence that I am deeply loved and understood by you. Help me fall in love with you, Abba Father."

Journal the Lord's voice in response to your prayer. Let Him ask you what you love. Maybe the two of you can start your own collection.

WRITING AND PAINTING BY JUSTINA STEVENS

COME
WIN
TER

WRITING AND INK SKETCH BY KEN HELSER

Growing up in the South, the greatest thrill of winter was when Mother would come to wake her three sons, pull back the curtain, blinding our sleepy eyes, then exclaim, "Look boys! Something happened last night!" We'd tear to the window, mesmerized by the beautiful white that had blanketed everything. We would squeal outrageously because school would be canceled, and snow meant, "Winter Holiday!"

We thought Mom was off her rocker when she'd pray before breakfast for all the poor folks who did not welcome the snow, but would be in danger. Where we lived in North Carolina, snow meant panic. Nobody knew how to drive in snow and ice, and just the mention of a wintry mix would send the masses to raid the grocery stores, leaving shelves empty—especially of milk and bread. While most of the South groaned at winter's cold, what mattered to the children was whether their seldom-used boots and gloves still fit. And the sled— "Where is it?"

A good snow is rare in the Deep South, and there have been none quite like the winter of 1963. That's when it snowed three Wednesdays in a row. It was a devastating time for a people totally lacking and ill-prepared for living without electricity, transportation or food. Many died during those weeks, while we children played. Vacation for three weeks meant amazing sledding. Loss of electricity meant adventure around fireplaces, roasting marshmallows, and sometimes whole families sleeping in one bed to keep warm. For children, winter snow meant a holiday of fun. Yet some storms leave a mark on us that is not forgotten.

Three deep snows followed by temperatures near zero shut down traffic. Fire and rescue operations could not get to those desperate for their aid. Many expectant mothers delivered their babies at home, while many elderly suffered severely without medication, warmth or food. Somehow in the storm's chaos, a mountain man deep in the wilds of the Blue Ridge Mountains was forgotten. When finally the old man was remembered, all knew it was too late for a rescue. Red Cross volunteers were called in to go and retrieve his dead body.

It took quite a team to plow through to the secluded area where he lived, and then, foot-by-foot, they dug a trail to his little cabin, hidden under a mountain of snow. Finally, after shoveling through snowdrifts up to ten feet high, they made a path to his door. Unfortunately the door was locked, but before going back to the rescue truck for an axe to cut through the door, someone laughed, "Why don't we try knocking?" In a half-hearted manner they knocked and called sarcastically, "Red Cross here." From inside the cabin there came a shocking sound—an old man's voice. A soft but firm voice, full of confidence, not fear. A voice so powerful that the knees of some buckled, and they had to hold to one another to keep from stumbling to the ground.

"Red Cross, eh? I've already given this year," the old man answered. "But since you've come such a long, hard way, why don't you come on in and warm a spell. Come, I'll make you some fresh coffee."

When they entered the cabin, they were amazed to find enough food, water and fuel stowed away to weather many winters. He had prepared for winter. He was one who survived the storm.

There's an old Proverb that should have been hanging on the wall of the mountain man's cabin: "When the storm has swept by, the wicked are gone, but the righteous stand firm forever" (Proverbs 10:25, NIV).

How do the righteous survive? Preparation.

A righteous man learns to live his life according to the four seasons of life. He knows spring is for planting, and the righteous man plants daily the good seed of God in his heart. Summer is for growing, and the righteous man tends the garden of his heart well, weeding and watering and caring for the plants so that when autumn comes, there is a great harvest of fruit. Life well lived. And that harvest is what brings on blessed winter, that season of rest in God that makes for the new seed of the Spirit to be planted come springtime. God's people. The prepared ones.

Recently I had the privilege of staying by the bed of my dying mother. I remembered her joyfully throwing open the curtains to reveal the new fallen snow. And I remembered her prayers for those whose lives might be destroyed by winter's cold. I thanked God that she managed to keep us warm around that little fireplace and never feared that the food would run out, because her pantry was always full of canned goods from past harvests. She had the boots already bought to fit our growing feet, and during spring, summer and fall had knitted brand new mittens to keep our little hands warm. And, yes, she knew exactly where that old Flexible Flyer sled was hidden in the basement.

Mother prepared for her final Winter of Eternal Rest, and peacefully died in my arms early in the morning. No fear. Just peace. And she lived a life preparing her husband, my siblings and me for our own final Winter. From her I gleaned life, and now I can say without hesitation, "Come winter..."

HEAVEN AND DUST

{ RECIPE FOR HONESTY WITH GOD }

God's first encounter with man was messy. Mud was on His hands after He formed us from the dust of the ground. Dirt was on His lips after He pressed His face against the clay and kissed us. Life began when God chose to get messy and kiss dust.

If life began with such a beautifully messy collision of Heaven and mud, why are we so afraid to be vulnerable and to get honest with God? We seem to waste so much time trying to give Him a flawless performance, when what He really desires is our broken and honest hearts. The Father is not afraid of our honesty and our mess. What if He is attracted to it? Look at the way the father ran down the road to embrace his prodigal son. This son had been homeless and living with pigs. I am sure you could smell him from a mile away. There was probably mud and pig waste caked over his whole body, but this didn't change the way the father embraced him. The Scripture says the father put his clean lips upon the dirty face of his son and kissed him with unfailing mercy. Just as the Father kissed mud in a garden and created man, this father kissed his prodigal and the son became a new man in his father's arms. Life comes from face-to-face encounters with the Father.

Going through the motions doesn't please you, a flawless performance is nothing to you. I learned God-worship when my pride was shattered. Heart-shattered lives ready for love don't for a moment escape God's notice.
Psalm 51:17-18, MSG

Psalm 51 reveals that God's desire is for a broken heart rather than a pristine sacrifice. What if God likes messy worship? Think about David dancing like a wild man and offering bloody sacrifices every six steps as they brought the Ark to Jerusalem. It was a glorious mess. Or imagine the bottle of perfume that Mary broke and poured over Jesus. These two worshipers touched God's heart like no one else in history. The worship they gave on this earth echoes into eternity. Jesus sits on the throne of David, and everywhere the gospel is preached, they talk about Mary's worship. God's heart is still longing for worshipers like these. The definition of worship in both Greek and Hebrew means to bow down and kneel in profound reverence. When we bow low in worship, we return to the place we came from: dust on the lips of God. Worship is the great restoring of Heaven and Earth. Worship is not a genre of music. Worship is a position of the heart. When you bow down, your heart rises over your head. In this place, with our knees touching the dust and our face pressed against the earth, we fall back into our first love—we return to our origin. Heaven and Earth kiss again.

Prompt: Take a piece of blank paper and find a place you can press your face against the earth. As your face touches the ground, feel your heart rise over your head. You are returning to the origin. Heaven has come to kiss the earth again. In this place, begin to pour out your heart to the Lord like Mary poured out her perfume. After you have poured out your heart, take some of the dirt that your face was pressed against and rub it into your blank piece of paper. Now on top of that dirt, write God an honest prayer from your heart. It can be a prayer of deep thanksgiving or a prayer of adoration. It can be a prayer of lamentation or a prayer of sorrow. It can be a beautiful prayer or a disheveled and jumbled prayer. Most importantly, let it be an honest prayer—your whole heart laid down on the dust. After you have finished, take a moment and read your prayer out loud to the Father, and then let His heart respond to you.

BY JONATHAN DAVID HELSER / PAINTING BY JUSTINA STEVENS

THE HUSH

WRITTEN BY MOLLY KATE SKAGGS
PHOTO BY JD GRAVITT

One of the loveliest things about winter is when the snow comes. The heart is irresistibly stirred within as if by a certain special kind of magic; the eye captures the wonderful sight of glittering flakes soaring upon the wintry winds, like each one had wings of her own. They gently fall from above and are soon gathered together until the whole earth is covered in the most beautiful blanket of quiet white. Many places in the world see much more snowfall than the woods of Sophia, North Carolina, and sure, snow definitely brings new elements of unpredictability and uncertainty with it. Yet it is sure to be said that every snow the earth has ever seen in her thousands of years must be more wondrous than the last. Snow is nothing short of a miracle—a gift from the Father of Lights, the Giver of all good and perfect gifts.

Have you ever noticed how everything gets still and quiet after a snowfall? There is a spectacular scientific wonder taking place here. Snowflakes are formed in many unique and beautiful sizes and shapes. Because of their individual patterns, falling snowflakes do not perfectly fit together when they land; rather, they build upon one another and collect in mounds. As a result of the accumulation, small open gaps form in between the snowflakes. Sound travels as invisible waves through the atmosphere, and as those waves pass over the piles of fallen snow, pressure squeezes them into those empty, hollow spaces. The sound waves are swallowed up by the heaps of freshly fallen snow! Loud, anxious noises are gone, and all we are left with is the hush in our ears. Everything around us sounds and feels quieter; everything seems to have slowed down and come to a place of stillness and rest. The air even smells cleaner. This acoustical phenomenon is also nothing short of a gift, a true wonder and miracle.

I believe that one of the many gifts the Lord loves to give to the world during winter seasons is that beautiful hush. I love sound and all things pertaining to sound. To me, one of the Father's greatest gifts to humanity is the ability to hear sound and perceive communication. So much is carried upon these incredible, unseen frequencies, such as information, intention, tone, color and emotion. Whether

it is a song, a laugh, the crackling of a fireplace or the winter winds, each sound is a window that gives us a look into God's nature. The hush after a snowfall carries a frequency all its own; it is a love letter right from the heart of God! Jesus said, "He who has ears to hear, let him hear" (Matthew 11:15, NKJV). He taught His disciples how to really see and hear the heart of His Father through everything around them by unveiling the miraculous Love of God through everyday moments. I would like to offer a perspective about winter that you may not have considered quite yet. The Holy Spirit has taught me so much through sound and music. He has shown me that if I would only open up my own heart and listen, I would find Him within those frequencies. A very wise man once said to me, "In everything, God has a voice," and I believe one of the Lord's favorite seasons to be heard and discovered in is the winter season. Winter is often misinterpreted as a cold, dark and lonely season in the year, as well as in the heart. Temperatures are painful, sometimes chilling you to the bone. The trees no longer hold the lush green life of spring, and it appears that the sun has taken a vacation. Yet if we had the eyes to see and ears to hear, we would be awakened to the unique and wondrous beauty the Father has to show us in winter.

God longs for us to hear His heart in everything around us, and His heart toward humanity was, is and always will be love. Whenever the snow falls, a window of the Father's heart opens up wide. Can you see His timeless message throughout the ages covering the earth in white redemption? His heart has always been to bring calm to the calamity, peace to the noise and rest to the anxiety. Each snowflake that falls is a kiss from the Father, a message from His heart to us. Can you hear Him? "I love you. You do not have to be afraid. The darkness is over and gone. I am your Father, and you are my forever-forgiven, beloved child." The kindness of His love covers the bare and helpless landscapes of our hearts and makes us, once again, beautiful to behold. The hate-filled voice of the enemy chatters on in a noisy, anxious mess of cacophony, filling our ears with lies about the Father and ourselves. But then, miracle of all miracles, his voice is swallowed up by the beautiful white grace and mercy that has piled upon our hearts in mounds of extravagance. Perfect Love has once again conquered until all that is left is the stillness. The quiet. The hush. And in the silence, our ears can clearly hear the voice of our Beloved: "Where are your accusers now? Joy to your world, for I have come. Receive the gift of peace I bring to you."

OUR COMPASS

{ RECIPE FOR TRUSTING THE WORD OF GOD }

When I was training to earn my open water SCUBA certification, I, along with several other students, had to learn about night diving. It was all about relying on the compass, being relaxed and learning to believe the tool in our hands. We had to learn this 100 feet down in the middle of a flooded rock quarry in the dark, cold water! Our instructor explained that when we had descended to the proper depth and safely gathered around the starting point—which was a buoyed rope—we would turn our lights off. Our only sense of direction would be our compass. Our instructor had one rule: we could not turn our lights on. If we did, we failed the course and would have to start over. When our instructor had everyone in place, all lights went out. I've never seen dark like that! The only illumination came from little glow sticks on our tanks so our instructor would not lose sight of us.

So I began: the buoyed rope, the start and finish line, eyes on the compass, ten kicks out, ninety degrees left turn—three times. It was perfectly quiet and dark and I felt how serious and important it was to stay focused on my compass. When I finished, my head hit the rope. It worked! It was true! The compass kept me from getting lost in the dark.

"Who among you fears the Lord and obeys the word of His servant? Let him who walks in the dark, who has no light, trust in the name of the Lord and rely on his God."
Psalm 51:17-18, NIV

The instructor was watching out for us all the entire time. He knew when a student needed help and when to give a student space to figure things out. There were many who missed the rope because they took their eyes off the compass and tried to look through the darkness to find their own way. When they tried to do it on their own, the instructor had to go and retrieve them.

The Word of God, the Bible, is our compass. It will always have a true reading. It always points in the correct direction. Likewise, the Holy Spirit is our instructor. He can always be trusted. I have watched through the years and seen friends who have taken their eyes off the Compass, the words of their Heavenly Father, and have wandered blindly through the dark instead of stopping and waiting on the help of the Holy Spirit to retrieve them.

Swimming in the dark required total trust. Just like my instructor required me not to light my own way and trust the compass, I must rely on God as my compass and not rely on my own strength. I have many times lit my own way and had to live through the consequences of my own immaturity. Let us trust the Lord with our whole hearts. Believe, embrace, love and have confidence in the Word, our Compass, and our Instructor.

Prompt: Read Proverbs 3:5-6, Psalm 119:105 and Psalm 139:23-24. Take a moment to open your heart and drink in the word of God. Ask the Holy Spirit to illuminate His word.

BY DAVID SHAVER

FRIEND

We have the greatest gift of friendship with the Holy Spirit. I love to think on the truth that we have a friend that sticks closer than a brother, and loves at all times. Remind your heart of these truths by reading Proverbs 18:24 and Proverbs 17:17.

Then take a few minutes and ask the Holy Spirit: "What is special about our relationship? Father, show me something wonderful about us." Wait and then journal His response to you. Read what He says a few times, and let it remind you about the great gift of friendship He has given you.

PROMPT BY KATELAND HILTY
PAINTING BY LINDSAY ARMISTEAD

THE GREAT MECHANIC

{ RECIPE FOR GOD'S MAINTENANCE }

My car has needed much mechanical work over the past year. I have listened to slight hiccups under the hood intensify into great gulps of air and sputter their last breaths. I have crossed my fingers, hoping problems would resolve themselves. I have asked for good mechanic recommendations and then finally swallowed the pricey pill of fixing my car. I have learned a great deal about car maintenance over these last months, namely the importance and great need we have for it. And inside a series of trips to the mechanic shop, I found the Lord.

You see, I had not just been visiting nearly every car mechanic shop in Sophia, I had been visiting The Great Mechanic, the one who offers the most important tune-up, the tuning of the heart. Reflecting on my tendencies in car maintenance inspired a revolutionary view into the way I tended my own heart. I am a frequent visitor of God's "car shop" and most days I casually drop by to tell Him what problems I am experiencing. Some internal clicking, an increasing grating sound, fingers crossed that each problem isn't too severe.

"Let me listen to it," He confidently woos me. I play Him the rhythms of my heart, sure to point out where it feels off, but He wants to see and hear for Himself.

"Lindsay, would you give me control of your heart?" He opens the driver's side door where I'm sitting and motions for the keys. So often I approach the Lord like He is an untrustworthy car mechanic, willing to take advantage of a girl who doesn't know enough about her car, doesn't know enough about her heart. I slow down, but I'm not ready to stop. I ask Him to listen but I don't trust what He hears. I may believe His diagnosis, but He is charging way too much.

"For He knows the secrets of the heart."
Psalm 44:21, ESV

In the middle of my mess, the Lord reminded me of a car mechanic I once met named Tony, who had the dirtiest face and hands I had ever seen. Tony's skin was so covered with grease and dust that I couldn't pick out any white spots except for the skin around his eyes. I asked Tony how long it takes him to wash up every evening. Tony just laughed. He wasn't committed to a clean face and hands. He was committed to clean cars. Underneath all the greasy grime and faded tattoos, I saw the face of another man in Tony. There was Jesus. The man who didn't care how much of a mess would be made when I requested a heart tune up. The man who bore the scars of my mess. The man committed to my whole, healthy heart.

I look up into the eyes of the man who knows my heart better than I do. He is not in a hurry. I hand over the keys and listen as He pops the hood. A steady, low hum surges from the depths of my soul and Jesus smiles. It is a good engine. It is a good heart.

Prompt: Slow down. Invite the Lord to listen to the rhythms of your heart. Imagine Him lifting the hood and smiling at the drumming of a healthy heartbeat. Ask the Lord where He sees a need for a tune-up and entrust Him with the keys of your heart. Journal His voice.

BY LINDSAY ARMISTEAD

WINTER PROMPT

PROMPT BY LUKE SKAGGS
PHOTO BY SYDNEE MELA

I used to think of winter as a mean old man who came around once every year to take away what was beautiful and worth seeing. If it were up to me, I'd be producing vibrant new leaves in every season. But that old man, in his wisdom, knows that if I had it my way, I would miss out. Every year he gently comes to remind me that it's time to rest. As I look around me, I see others just like me, standing in their desperate wiry frames in a backdrop of winter's pure white covering, and I'm reminded of my truest beauty. The beauty of my life is not measured by what I can produce, but by how I stand firm through every season, rooted in the rich deep soil of the Father's love. Often times, it's hard for us to remember who we are or what we look like outside of our accomplishments or when there's nothing hanging from our branches.

Take some time and sit with Father. Ask, "Holy Spirit, would you show me who I am beyond the work of my hands, my temporal leaves?" He would love to show you the consistency of Jesus in your life. Journal His voice in response to you.

Let's go fly a kite

WRITTEN BY JONATHAN HELSER
PHOTOGRAPHY BY MELISSA HELSER

"MY FAVORITE PART OF COMING HOME FROM A TRIP IS WALKING THROUGH THE FRONT DOOR AND BEING ATTACKED BY MY CHILDREN'S KISSES. I LOVE TELLING THEM THERE IS A GIFT HIDDEN IN MY SUITCASE AND THEN WATCHING THEM FRANTICALLY UNZIP MY BAGS LOOKING FOR IT."

There is something incredible about God asking you a question. Each time I have experienced this, I am overcome with a mixture of joy and awe. I feel the joy of being pursued by a Friend who really wants to know me, for a great friend is always more interested in you than himself. A true friend knows how to ask the kind of questions that help you discover more of who you are. True friends sincerely care more about what's happening in your world than theirs. I am filled with awe when God pursues me in this way, because it is a staggering thought that an all-knowing God would humble Himself to my level and ask me for an answer. Does He really not know the answer? Or does He want me to see something I have never seen before? God's questions echo His pursuit in Eden when He called out to His children: "Where are you?" I don't think God lost us; He just wanted us to find Him and remember who we were. His questions reveal how relational He is. They are never meant to condemn us or accuse us. They are intended to call us back to the place of walking with Him hand-in-hand as Adam did in Eden.

Recently, in the middle of a very mundane moment, God invaded my space and asked me this question: "When you were a boy, what was the greatest gift your dad gave you for Christmas?" It was such an out-of-the-box question that I knew I was in a burning-bush moment, so I took off my shoes and engaged the question with all my heart. I started running through files of memories from Christmases gone by: stockings filled with candy, balls, bats, Nintendo games, GI Joes, sweaters, socks. And then it struck me...the BB gun. That was it. Undoubtedly, that was my favorite gift he ever gave me. I still have that spring-action Daisy BB gun with a solid wood headstock. I have taught my son and daughter how to shoot with that gun. But why in the world would God interrupt my day to ask me such a random question? What does a BB gun have to do with a God who has much bigger things to think about than my Christmas gift from over twenty years ago?

But then I heard that beautiful, still small whisper say, "The BB gun was your favorite gift because the gift required your father's presence." Suddenly I remembered the look on my mom's face when I opened the gift. She was shocked (and a bit terrified) that her eight-year-old boy had a weapon. She quickly blurted out: "Ken, I told you I didn't want him to have a BB gun till he was at least ten years old. He is not allowed to use that gun without your constant supervision." This gift was going to require my father's constant presence, or else I couldn't even use it. This little gun prepared the way for the best Christmas I had ever had. My dad and I spent that entire Christmas holiday together.

My dad taught me how to load the gun and cock the gun, how to apply the safety and how to take care of it. He came down to my level and taught me how to look through the sights to aim at the target. We had shooting contests with old tin cans. We roamed the woods like cowboys, terrorizing all the squirrels of our forest. The gift was much more than a piece of metal and wood. The gift was a space to connect with my dad. My dad became like a little boy with each shot he took, and I became a little bit more like a man each time I fired the gun. The gift gave me friendship with my father.

Last winter Melissa and I were on a ministry trip in Boulder, Colorado. We had an afternoon off, and we were taking a stroll on Pearl Street in downtown Boulder. As we were walking through this amazing town, Melissa squeezed my hand and said, "Let's get the kids an amazing gift." As soon as she said this, we saw a shop devoted entirely to kites. We headed directly to the shop and purchased the most fantastic kite we could find for the kids.

My favorite part of coming home from a trip is walking through the front door and being attacked by my children's kisses. I love telling them there is a gift hidden in my suitcase and then watching them frantically unzip my bags looking for it. When they unwrapped their amazing new kite from this trip, they were so excited that they wanted to fly it right then, but it was already way past their bedtime. The next day our trees were swaying in the wind. Although it was the middle of winter, it was a perfect day to fly a kite. It was just cold enough that a coat felt like a warm embrace. We bundled up and found this wonderful field close to our home. As we walked out into the beauty of the open space, my children's eyes were on me. It was one of those father moments when you feel like their hero, when you know they need you and they want to be with you. They followed me through the field with simple childlike wonder. I suddenly realized this gift was just like the BB gun. My children had never flown a kite quite like this, and they couldn't use the gift without their father. Just as the kite is useless without the wind, this gift required my presence for it to fly. We assembled the kite and attached the string. We lifted it into the wind and it magically danced out of our hands into the sky. I watched my son and daughter, filled with delight, and I felt my heart soaring with the kite. We ran back and forth across the field as if the kite were pulling us somewhere we had never been before. Through this little kite, I was seeing things I had never seen before. The kite would maybe last a few years, but my kids would carry this moment for the rest of their lives. As the string unraveled, letting the kite fly higher, my heart was being unraveled with the truth of what makes gifts wonderful. My heart was being unraveled from the knots and lies that have kept me from enjoying the gifts the Father of fathers has given me. So many times I run away with the gifts He has given me. I try to figure them out all on my own, like an orphan clutching the gift with a fear that it will be taken away. I think that I must perform to keep the gift. I think I must use the gift to earn my place in the world. I have looked at the gift to give me identity, instead of looking to my Father to define me. But as I watched the kite reach higher into the sky, my heart saw the love of a Father who only gives good and perfect gifts—gifts that require His presence to fly.

TWO PIECES
of DRY LAND

WRITTEN BY CHRIS MILLER
PHOTOGRAPHY BY DAVID BURBACH

It was a crisp October weekend when I set off with five close guy friends for an epic camping trip on the North Carolina coast. We hooked a sailboat up to our big white van and stuffed it full of sleeping bags, lanterns, warm clothes and coolers full of hearty snacks and campfire meals. We were to launch our vessel and sail to a small island thirteen miles from the dock where we would camp and enjoy quality time as brothers. We made it to the coast within a few hours and dropped our brave sailboat into the water. My friends had charted an amazing course that none of us had attempted before. Everything about this trip would be new for me. I was thrilled to be invited on my first sailing adventure—and slightly nervous. As we pushed off from the dock and into the blue, I could feel anxiety starting to creep in, but I pushed it aside. I couldn't ask for better company, and I trusted our captain.

And so we set off, six lanky fellows in a humble nineteen-foot vessel. Space was a luxury on our little boat. We had a limited window of daylight to make it out of the harbor, into the ocean and onto the island before nightfall, and at first, we didn't seem to be moving quickly. Regardless, joy filled our sails as the wind and the waves started to pick up, and we sailed onward to our destination.

It was a longer trip than I expected, and with six grown men onboard, there wasn't much room to move around. After an hour or so, the bobbing motion of our tiny boat began to shake me up a bit. I realized how vulnerable it is to be a passenger on a small sailboat. A few times, the wind changed directions pretty rapidly, and we had to shift the sides we were sitting on to adjust the weight in the boat. One time it happened so quickly that our vessel dipped thirty-five degrees to one side and gave our bottoms a nice dunk in the icy cold seawater, which made for a very chilly ride the rest of the way! It was of small comfort to me to learn that the keel on the sailboat makes it nearly impossible to capsize, but I had never been on a boat with this much lean, and this was no leisurely trip across the lake. This was real sailing, and there were moments that were uncomfortable. I found myself pining for the shore, and even anxiously looking towards our destination, waiting to be off the ride and out of the boat. When a lighthouse finally came into view, I felt assurance wash over me, and I fixed my eyes on that point. And even though some of my best friends were right beside me, my heart was no longer fully in the boat. The closer we got, the more I yearned to be out of the water and onto dry land. I felt great comfort in that lighthouse and my fantasy of a warm and cozy campsite.

It was getting dark when we were finally able to make out the island. My heart sunk when I realized that the lighthouse was not our actual destination but merely a fixed point. All of this time, I had built up an idea of what our campsite would look like, and I was picturing a tame harbor. The lighthouse simply stood as a source of light to help guide us into the cove where we would be camping, and that was where the true adventure really began. Our campsite would be established whenever and wherever we could manage to anchor our boat. There were no lights, no wooden docks and no easy answers. There in that sandy cove our humble vessel was battered by Northeasterly winds as we tried desperately to anchor our boat and wade with our supplies to the sandy shore. I witnessed a moment that made my heart skip a beat when one of our guys was knocked over by the main sail that whipped from one side of the boat to the other. He fell onto the wooden tiller, breaking it in half. We were bobbing around like a toy boat in a bathtub with no easy way to steer or motor our way out of our position. It was quite thrilling! Finally, two of the boys expertly managed to secure our boat with two anchors as the rest of us jumped over the side and stood waist-deep in the frigid water, forming a human chain to pass our supplies safely to the shore. For me, that first step onto dry land felt like a miracle. I was astonished at the way everyone joyfully worked together to establish camp in soggy clothes and empty bellies. Hours later, as we huddled around one of the most comforting campfires of my life, I realized what an amazing privilege it was to be on that island. I looked around at the faces of my friends and felt immensely thankful to be on such an adventure with them. Just a few hours before, I had felt uncomfortable enough to have happily turned around, jumped back in our van and headed to some safe place. But in that moment, I didn't want to be anywhere else. Had we turned back, or had I turned down the opportunity to go sailing in the first place, I would have missed out on a beautiful adventure with some of the most courageous men I knew.

A wise man once said to me, "You can get frustrated in the middle of the journey, wanting the destination. But remember the journey *is* the destination." I think about this now and laugh to myself. I think about that sailing trip and what happened between the dock and the shore. It seems to me that sailing, just like all of life, is about the journey. We can live like we are waiting for something, anything, and miss out on what the Father has for us right now. I learned something about being present on that sailing trip with those five brothers. My Father wanted to give me a good gift in that trip. The adventure strengthened our friendship and knit our hearts closer together. The most significant part of that trip was not the camping, the glorious fire or the great meals we shared. It was what happened in our hearts on the journey, and how we fought for one another along the way. It was about giving in to the process. It was never about the destination. It was about every moment in between two pieces of dry land.

"MY NEEDINESS
FOR GOD IS MY
HONOR AND NOT
MY SHAME."

-JD GRAVITT

Roots Run Deep

Peace settles in like a blanket draped around my shoulders. Removing my boots, I'm greeted by smiles and hellos calling me into the kitchen. Jonathan is making a cup of coffee for Melissa like he does every morning, and Melissa is sitting at their kitchen table making easy conversation, occasionally brightening the space with effortless laughter. It's an ordinary day—a Monday—but a magical feeling rests in the room.

WRITTEN BY ALLIE SAMPSON
PHOTOGRAPHY BY JD GRAVITT

I remember experiencing this feeling when I walked into this house for the first time in the summer of 2012. It was during The 18 Inch Journey, and Jonathan and Melissa invited our entire school up to their house for an Open Mic Night. When I came through their front door, I was immediately enamored with the simple beauty of their house. The colors were inviting, the lighting was soothing and an aroma of fresh coffee welcomed me in. But more than anything, what delighted me was the feeling that greeted me: the feeling of home. The walls were elegantly decorated with pictures of their family, paintings created by friends and various instruments. A white cubed shelving unit was filled in with books and artifacts of an adventurous and valued life together. The walls of their home whispered a simple truth to me: this was a family in love.

Now, sitting down in the same house that mesmerized me only a few years ago, I realize that the magical feeling of home that continuously greets me at the door of the Helser house is something that they have cultivated—something they have fought for. As their Personal Assistant, I have had many moments of closely observing Jonathan and Melissa. I have sat beside them at both weddings and funerals. I have been a little-known acquaintance, and I have lived in their basement. I've watched from the back of a packed auditorium as

they lead hundreds of people into the depths of the heart of God, and I have seen them covered in dirt and sweat while tending the land of A Place for the Heart. I have seen them both at a distance and at close-range, and the contrast of the circumstances I have seen them in has served to highlight this theme: they are remarkably consistent—their roots run deep.

Making our way to their front porch, they offer me a latte and put a variety of snacks on a small, round table. Melissa leans into the wicker couch, and the wisteria that frames the porch hangs above Jonathan as he sits back into a chair. As they settle in, they begin to unpack the story of how they fell in love and what their journey has looked like. Jonathan and Melissa are fourteen years into marriage. They met in ministry school, and Jonathan affectionately recounts the tale of quickly becoming friends, and Melissa going on a trip to Scotland soon after they met. A smile captures his face as he recalls making a Kevin Prosh mix-tape for her and anxiously anticipating the day that she would be back in class. They began dating just a little while later and fell in love quickly. Melissa mentions that what intrigued her so much about Jonathan was his gentleness and the contrast it was to her more passionate personality. She smiles at her husband as she describes how different they are and the way that has extracted the best out of both of them: "We realized very quickly that we had two very different dreams, but we were both rooted and grounded in the love of the Lord. And now they make sense. I'd say Jonathan's gentleness has wooed me into knowing how to be still and really know the Lord. His ability to process through song really intrigued me and taught me how to love the Lord in a way that I didn't know how. And on the flip side, I invited Jonathan into understanding that to love the Lord is to love people. To live life fully is not to be isolated or smothered, but it is the tension of all of it. I know I've taught him how to be loved by the Lord through people while he has taught me to be still and just be loved by the Lord."

I let my heart pause and settle into her statement: "But we were both rooted and grounded in the love of the Lord." Her words wash over me, and I am drenched in their truth. Instantly, my mind is flooded with stories from their journey. They have seen the expanse of weather that life brings—the serenity of sunny days and the turmoil of raging storms—and they have withstood it. Somehow, in the midst of storms and winter seasons, their roots sunk deeper and their trust and dependence on the Holy Spirit grew. Melissa begins to tell me about her sickness as she remembers seasons of surgery and suffering: "Since the beginning of our marriage, we have walked through the tension of my sickness; we were kind of hurled into a storm. When I look back on it now, probably the most encouraging thing is seeing that the Lord was so present, but even more than that, that we *knew* that the Lord was present. It wasn't just that I could see Him working, but that now, when I look back, I can see that we saw the Lord working in those moments, and you don't always get that privilege when you're in the middle of such crazy, intense suffering. The extreme sorrow brought us face-to-face with a part of the Lord that not many people get to see. The assurance that people see when they look in our eyes when we're together comes from crazy wilderness seasons that could have taken us out, but didn't—because we had made a choice to see the goodness of the Lord no matter what. As I look back, it is astounding to me that we were so sure of the goodness of the Lord in the midst of everything that was happening. But I know that what we're giving our lives to now…well, I'm not sure if we could be leading it if we hadn't gone through that season."

Jonathan adds: "The journey of the winter seasons was causing our roots to go deep enough to hold the weight of the fruit that was coming in the Promised Land. I know now that some of the promises we are walking in are being sustained by the depths of our roots that were established in wilderness seasons."

As we continue talking, I'm astonished by how much wisdom keeps coming from them on such a wide array of topics. They speak with authority and gratitude, and their words are marked with honor and courage. It is from this place, surrounded by their wisdom, that I try to unpack everything that they've said; but as I try to assess each statement's value, I see that each revelation is the fruit of their life together. None of their encouragement or insight, none of their teachings or songs, none of their revelation or inspiration would be possible if they had not chosen the Father in winter seasons and allowed Him to grow their roots deeper in confidence and trust.

They talk openly and candidly about their valleys low, but they are just as vocal about the mountains high. The two begin to recount sweet memories from leading thousands in worship to running Phase I and Phase II of The 18 Inch Journey to intimately discipling members of the core staff at A Place for the Heart, who have lived on the land for years. Melissa's face is swept up in a thought-provoking assurance as she explains: "We have the great privilege of doing lots of different forms of ministry—leading worship, conferences, schools, leading the eight and the thousands. And I think that, to come to this stage in our life and still really love it all proves that if you give yourself fully to loving Jesus, then He so brilliantly gives you capacity to love the way He loves." Jonathan glances at Melissa and echoes her sentiment by expounding on how they have come to measure success. "Our measuring stick for success is how much family is being produced in a ministry. The more Heaven comes to Earth, the more Earth will look like family. I'm more in love with Jesus than I was fourteen years ago. Ministry is amazing and we are still having so much fun, and I consider that to be one of our greatest successes."

We go on talking until sundown, marveling at the faithfulness of God and His profound provision and kindness in the Helsers' lives. As we're wrapping up our conversation, I recall all of the things we've just talked about: parenting, family, ministry, discipleship, hard seasons, choosing joy, falling in love and marriage. I look them both in the eyes and ask a simple question, "Is it worth it?" Melissa leans back, her face glowing with peace and confidence. "Knowing that something is worth it, for us, is when we step back and realize that we've never been so needy for the Lord. That's the crown on a season."

As the sun begins to set, I lace up my boots, tell the Helsers goodnight and set off back down the trail through the woods. Surrounded by a mass of trees, I pause to look up and stand in awe of their height. "In order for you to grow tall, you must first grow deep—your roots must be able to support you," I whisper to the forest. This same secret I give to the trees is what I have identified in Jonathan and Melissa. They have grown tall because they have let Love sink their roots deep.

Shame Personified

WRITTEN BY JD GRAVITT

The one-eyed man with sailored breath sauntered over to me with the intention of a walking buzzard. He smiled at me with a sparsely-toothed grin. He smelled like microphone feedback and looked like the dish sink after a great feast. Time seemed irrelevant to his person except for what had been, but was no longer. He and his yellow grin walked right up to me like the words in a dictionary. He held my name in his mouth like an after-dinner toothpick.

Himself in shambles, he presented himself as a representation of my character. He cocked his head, shoulders straight underneath the dingy blue and brown stained suit coat. I recognized the trash he carried in his briefcase as my mail I thought the garbage men had collected. He held the trash like a verdict and his face shone with enticement.

Who was this mockery of a man, and how did my name get in his mouth? How did he find me in my home as I sat down to eat? In his right hand he took my plate of food, and in his left he placed a court subpoena in front of me. Only, it wasn't a court subpoena. In front of me lay all the sins of my life catalogued in chronological order. I flipped through boatloads of my lowest moments from the playground to arguments with my parents. Next to each sin was a guilty verdict.

As I read, the man began walking around my house taking my pictures off the wall. He carried a large canvas bag behind him and started placing the joys of my life inside the bag. Then he began to pour white Elmer's glue on the floor. He stepped in it, smearing the mud from his boots into a milky brown slime. Acting as a great artist, the man flung himself into a dance, painting the walls of my house with the bottom of his boots.

He unraveled my trash, smoothing it against his chest and officially pasting it to my walls. Then he pulled a pack of photos from his jacket and decorated the walls with them. These pictures documented each of my catalogued sins. This left me looking at all I had ever done with the smell of drying glue in my nose. Then he was gone.

––––––––––––––––––––

Shame seems like such a subtle enemy, similar to having a cold. My normal response to shame is often a shrug of the shoulders, but I wanted to expose the sinister agenda of shame. Shame cripples our self-worth and keeps us from living whole-hearted lives. Our heavenly Father tells us we are worth Jesus, but shame tells us that there is something about us that is not worthy of love. Shame is like a cancer for the courage of our hearts, paralyzing us in fear and keeping us from our full inheritance as children of God.

My desire is that you would leave this story with a greater understanding of the redemption of Jesus in your life. I think it's easy to skip over the power of grace when we don't fully understand the poison of shame. I've grown up believing that Jesus set me free from sin, and it's easy for me to diminish His redemption as a nice thing done by a nice guy. The overwhelming power of grace comes when we see the overwhelming hopelessness of our sin. What would it look like if someone came into your house and rearranged things so that you had to face all your shortcomings? This is what shame does to us. Simply naming shame removes the crippling power of deception and condemnation from our lives.

"When we were utterly helpless, Christ came at just the right time and died for us sinners" (Romans 5:6, NLT).

Right now, you may find yourself with some unresolved places in your heart, places defiled with the dirt and glue of shame. I pray that you would feel the great grace of Jesus wrap around you in your most helpless state. I pray that His arms of unconditional love would hold and comfort you. He has paid the price for all of your sins so that you can live in freedom. He wants to trade you His righteousness for all the wrong you've ever done. I pray that you would make the exchange and receive the full adoption as a son or daughter of God. You are free and no longer a slave to your former life; you are a child of God. In Jesus' name. Amen.

TO TAME A TEMPEST | BY ALLIE SAMPSON

He caught me.
When I could not catch my breath,
Breath caught me,
With kind eyes—smiled and asked
May I tame your tempest?

Reluctantly I looked.
His silver irises resembled my storm
Yet, rather than upheaval, in them I found
Myself
Fatigue unfurled a quiet *yes*

Closer He came
To tame a tempest, you must first untangle it, He said
And gently began unraveling doubts from my hair
He wove trust into my tresses,
Braided belonging around my crown

He took my hand.
To tame a tempest, you must tether it, He sang
And stitching His fingers into mine
He sewed friendship into my depths,
Banished abandonment from my borders

He looked into my eyes.
To tame a tempest, you must look at it, He whispered
And locking eyes with mine,
Silver pierced blue
Securing bravery behind understanding
Silence approached
Rest reintroduced itself
But horizons held secrets of
Brooding monsoons

Chaos crashed against me
Tumult intruded upon me
Breakers berated me
Hold your Breath! they taunted
Lest He escape you.

I searched for silver but only saw grey.
I contested
You spoke peace!
Yet wind still howls like mountain's wolf
And sea still swirls like raven's flock!
Did not you tame my tempest?

Breath answered:
To whom does the sea surrender?
For whom will the wind unwind?
Have I not named you tempest's tamer?

Touch our tresses' trust
Feel our friendship's fingers
See the stifled storm

To tame a tempest, He smiled,
we must tame it together.

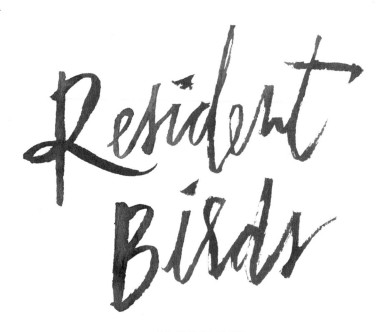

Resident Birds

BY ERIN GRAVITT

North Carolina had a particularly long and unusual winter last year. I lost count of the number of times businesses and roads closed down due to unexpected ice pellet storms, sleet and freezing rain. The South is a bit helpless without tire chains and an abundance of snow plows—not fully prepared with snow equipment like the North is. A whole city can shut down due to threats of frost. Icy, dangerous road conditions make it impossible for drivers to get out of their driveways; I can regrettably testify to spinning car wheels in gray sludge for longer than I'd like to admit.

When we frustratingly look out our frozen windows and see endless, dreary sleet, and the pine trees weighed down with ice, it can be easy to wish we were in a warmer, easier season. One that is more convenient. One that has easy access to whatever we want. Then, a question for the Lord: Why make this season more difficult? Let's take a lesson from the birds.

When it comes to birds, many migrate when the signs of winter's scarcity and chilliness start showing. They need greater accessibility to food and warmth. However, there are a few birds that do not migrate. They are called resident birds. They are the Muhammad Ali's and George Washington Carver's of the bird world. Instead of migrating, blackbirds have learned to protect their home and food source by removing snow with twigs. Doves and bullfinches adapt their diet, trying things they may have never eaten before in order to survive.

Who needs to be a fair-weather friend when your God-given ingenuity makes for the abundant life? How amazing that birds have such natural adaptability! People are the same. We are constantly being tested and restructured by variations in our lives, which the Lord kindly creates for us that we may truly change, mature, adapt and grow. Starvation and death are not our portion in winter seasons in the natural or of the heart. Not only has the Lord given us what we need to survive, but also He supplies us with what we need to flourish and thrive in the harshest of winters. Different seasons call for different actions. In winter seasons, choice is our greatest action. We must choose to exploit a new food source or be ready to clean up our house to make it cozy. Make a decision to be persistent and smart. Look into the face of the Lord and see the provision in His eyes for you. He makes us competent. He has given us the gift of choosing Him, and when spring comes, the strength that was forged in the winter is evident.

If you have a *please-God-send-warm-weather* kind of day, remember the birds that stayed. They stayed, they modified, they grew in their resourcefulness. And when spring came, they were more alive. The Lord rewards us when we choose to stay and endure and persevere through the severe, bitter winter of the soul. He wants to be something so special to us even now, when we feel cold, miffed, lethargic and inconvenienced in our hearts and minds. He loves us and stays warm-hearted toward us in every season. Our love, character and relationship with Him are able to overflow after tough terms when we hold fast. When the sun breaks and the spring light comes, we will be thankful for what only winter could give us.

Prompt: Write a prayer of thankfulness to God in your journal. Thank Him for the opportunity to choose Him in every season. Thank Him for your choice to choose Him every day. Open your eyes and see the strength He is wielding in your heart.

LET HIM HEAR YOUR GENTLE WHISPERS

POEM BY ERIN GRAVITT
ILLUSTRATION BY JUSTINA STEVENS

Let Him hear Your gentle whispers
When the drunks and demons jeer
At the successes and failures alike; disperse
Your pacifying light, beaming warm and dear.
His childlike feebleness resting on paternity
Is His glory not His shame;
For what sane father, with odd uncertainty,
Would ever hesitate, for the babe of
His blood, to give his own name?
No doubts are now needed,
Not even a slight bit;
Nor will they be necessary
Tomorrow or the next day.
The voice you long to hear passes
By your cave's mouth,
And your ears perk at the familiar,
"Child, you are my favorite."
You know—you do know
He will keep your enemies at bay;
He will remain with you ever in Winter's
Death when the geese fly south.

Cutting Wood

WRITTEN BY JAKE J STEVENS
PHOTO BY SYDNEE MELA

It felt like we were in another world, over there across the road. It was a massive tract of land that had been clear cut to sell off as lots full of acres. For weeks, JD Gravitt and I had the pleasure of gearing up most every morning to face the cold of winter to cut firewood for the farm. I am pretty sure those days of cutting, splitting and stacking are a huge reason we are where we are today. We might as well have been at war the way we talked. It felt as if we were eight thousand miles away on some distant battlefield. Talks of love and marriage, of growing old and of being real men filled our mouths and our ears as our warm breath filled the cool air. Those are important days in my heart, and if you asked JD, I am sure he would say the same. Even now, whenever there is an eternal moment that takes place, usually one of us will mention "those days when we cut wood" and say that it somehow made way for this present moment to happen, whatever the moment may be. Recently for each of us it was a wedding, getting married to the women of our dreams. Next it will be having kids, and then later being grandparents, I'm sure. I know I make it sound glorious, like we were in a war and we won, but in a way we really were in a war, and we did win. Those cold winter days couldn't contend with the fire that began to burn in our hearts as we dreamed about becoming the kind of men who would do anything for their wives someday. Along with the conversations, the victory was the work of our hands, it was being given a job and seeing it through to the end. It was having a good attitude and a good position of the heart. Chopping wood was the perfect place to put into practice what our hearts were dreaming about. We learned a lot about how to take initiative and make decisions over there. Most importantly, I believe a vision was cast in our hearts to become the men we heard about in stories and the heroes we saw in movies. Even more than that, we dreamed of becoming the kind of men who really made a difference, who were as bold as lions and confident and fierce in the face of our enemies. We dreamed of becoming men who could lead, protect and provide for the loves of their lives. We dreamed of becoming men of God. I would say that JD and I have both become those things and will continue to become those things till the day we breathe our last.

"Where there is no vision, the people perish..." Proverbs 29:18, KJV

Prompt: Those years ago, my battlefield was choosing to work hard and diligently in the cold cutting wood, wood that I might never use myself. Those hours of labor and choosing a good attitude set the scene for me to dream for my life. What battlefield are you avoiding in your life where the Lord wants you to dream something great? Sometimes the greatest victory is in your choosing to say yes to the Lord where you are at. There He will meet you and forge character in your heart and inspire you to become something great. Dare to say yes and become something and someone even greater than you already are! Write down your battlefield, and then repent to the Father for avoiding His fullness for you on that battlefield. Then say yes next time you're out there and receive what the Father has!

WINTER GARDEN

A cold wind blows in as a chilling reminder that autumn has passed and the seasons are changing once again. The last of the leaves have fallen off the trees, leaving their tall silhouettes to mark the once-dense tree line next to the garden. Winter in the garden holds a stark contrast to summer's blazing heat, buzzing insects and bright produce. It's quiet, the bugs and other pests have gone into hibernation and the sun is low and cool. Left to the elements, not much will grow past late autumn; however, with careful tending, it can produce an abundant harvest. The winter garden takes forethought because the gardener must plant cold hardy crops, like kale and carrots, while the sun is still hot and the trees are dense with leaves. If these plants are given the time and nourishment to grow in the warm months, they will be able to maintain growth throughout the winter months. Every vegetable thrives in season; carrots grown in summer are like tomatoes grown in winter—bland and lifeless. The harvest of this season is marked by the curly green leaves of kale, the sweetness of carrots and the robust beauty of beets. These nutrient-dense plants were created to thrive, and become even sweeter and more delicious as they adapt to the cool and then cold temperatures.

Winter is the time for the garden to strengthen and protect what it's already growing, not to lay desolate, void of life and growth until spring returns. Because even one hard freeze could be their end, even the hardiest of plants are in need of a gardener. Like the physical garden, the garden of our heart is tended by a good Gardener to be full of life in every season. Sometimes the fruit is bright and growth happens quickly. However, in other seasons, the fruit grows slowly and the change appears gradually. Even in patient growth, the winter produces a harvest more nutrient dense than any other season. Remarkably, the cruciferous vegetable family—which includes broccoli, kale, cabbage, etc.—are considered by scientists to be the most nutrient dense of all vegetables, and these grow best in cold seasons.

"As the rain and the snow come down from heaven, and do not return to it without watering the earth and making it bud and flourish, so that it yields seed for the sower and bread for the eater, so is my word that goes out from my mouth: It will not return to me empty, but will accomplish what I desire and achieve the purpose for which I sent it."
Isaiah 55:10-11, NIV

The garden of my own heart has seen many seasons. I have seen the good Gardener intentionally plant what will thrive in each season. At times I have found myself determined to produce tomatoes in winter. Discouraged that no growth is happening, I turn inward and try to find what I have done wrong. Yet in His kindness, the great Gardener has taken my hand and led me away from the barren tomato bed to show me the abundance of life thriving in another part of my garden. I've seen trust in the Gardener grow and been filled with the nutrients to sustain me even in the coldest days.

Prompt: Picture your heart as a beautiful garden blessed by winter. Look deeper and see the Master Gardener's great attention to each plant, choosing varieties that will thrive in your heart and bring nourishment to your soul. Read Isaiah 55:10-12 and see God's great intentionality with your heart. In your journal, ask the Master Gardener what He has planted in your heart this season and how you can tend it together. Journal His voice, and then craft a prayer of thanksgiving for your heart.

WRITING AND PAINTING BY EMILY PELL

A MAN VOID OF THE SPIRIT — THE NATURAL
MAN — HAS TO UNDERSTAND IN ORDER TO
BELIEVE, BUT THE SPIRITUAL MAN BELIEVES
IN ORDER TO UNDERSTAND.

-KEN HELSER

Handmade

a feature on CREATIVITY,
the TRINITY *and* JUSTINA STEVENS

Written by Erin Gravitt
Photography by JD Gravitt

She is not in a rush. Natural instincts. Big, calm eyes and a lovely face. She exudes effortlessness and honesty. We sit together in the Art Barn on what feels like one of the last days of summer. Falling acorns make loud, abrupt *tonk* sounds on the tin roof above us as she folds thick, white paper with a cow-bone folder. She is not in a rush. Deftly moving hands have prepared a stack of paper in advance. She is making a small, leather-bound journal that embraces earthy excellence. It is beautifully rough around the edges—literally. She punches small holes in the weathered, rich brown leather covering with an awl. She will cleverly sew the binding in less than an hour, back-tracking only once after a mis-poke with her needle. Mistakes don't faze her. She is not in a rush. The atmosphere around her feels unmoved and soft. She takes her time and speaks with a voice like a Parisian hand-turned music box, a song of sighing and smiling in stillness.

Justina Brinkley Stevens is newly married and on top of the world. She is an art teacher and authentic lover of handmade craft. She inspires and challenges staff and students alike at A Place for the Heart to pursue and refine their creative process. She was raised as a dancer, following in the footsteps of her august mother. Her father was a brilliant businessman, so the creative process runs deep in her DNA. Her grandmothers used to knit, crochet and create dollhouses, and they even won state fair craft competitions. When Justina was sixteen years old, she became the heir to all of Grandma Jeanne's art supplies, and that is when her journey into hand-craftsmanship took flight. "If I didn't have anything to do with my hands, I would explode," Justina says with a sure grin on her face.

Throughout her ten years of hand-making articles of various shapes and forms—pieces of jewelry, paintings, drawings and journals, among other things—the Lord has been a committed friend and companion. At school, work and home, she consistently found the Lord in the quiet places and craved the Holy Spirit's steadfast stillness. She still does today. The striking, grounded craftswoman opens up about what the comforting voice of the Lord has sounded like for her over the years when she is creating: "Without fail I hear Him say, 'Justina, I don't need a thing from you. What I would like is to share a space with you and to be quiet.'" And that is the very key to her heart. She feels the Lord lean in, in a way that tames her heart. No words are needed. It is a settling place. God enjoys those quiet moments with us. "If the Lord does say something," Justina adds, "He will kindly compare my season to what I am making and bring understanding to my life."

As I watch Justina fluently work, I wonder about so many of us who feel jaded, frustrated and clueless when we try and approach the creative process. Perhaps we feel stuck, unsure of where to start when it comes to painting, drawing, sculpting, knitting, welding, building, you name it. Sometimes creating with our hands and hearts seems like a vicious trap. We get caught up in making something look perfectly attractive for someone's stamp of approval. We yearn to hear the praise and applause of anyone—a parent, friend, colleague, professor or critic. We become crushed under the weight of criticism and comparison. Where does our fear of creating come from? Perhaps part of it is that we are putting our blood, sweat and tears into a product that represents us. This is exposing and vulnerable; the fear can be real.

Justina kindly combats this purgatory paradigm with a clear statement of truth and faith: "You've been taught a lie and have believed that you aren't worthy

"YOU WON'T BE MONET, PICASSO OR CEZANNE.
YOU WILL BE YOU.
THAT IS WHERE YOU WANT TO LAND."

of creating. Just try. Try making things for the sake of doing something new and fun. Collaborate with the Lord. That's a great place to start." Herein lies the invitation to pause and remember the ease and joy of friendship with God.

Take a breath, and listen carefully: Don't imagine what you're making for other people. Ask yourself, "For whom am I intending the work of my hands?" If you're doing it for others, you'll be disappointed. If you're doing it to be close to the Lord, then there's no need to fear failure when you're with the Friend that loves at all times. The light that chases away the creeping darkness of fear is simple. "Settle into the realization that you are just a person," shrugs Justina. "You won't be Monet, Picasso or Cézanne. You will be you. That is where you want to land." It's not true that to begin you must achieve. What debilitating pressure! Our relationship with Jesus isn't like that. Why should our creative process be like that? This quiet, creative place is real and attainable for anyone, regardless of if we believe we are "artistic" or "a creator." Creativity isn't exclusive to a group of certain elite people; it is an incredible gift and right from God for all of humanity. It is for us. It is for you.

Creativity is an invitation to learn with grace and patience. Justina imagines Jesus learning from His father, Joseph, (and His Abba) about how to be a carpenter and what helpfulness and benevolence must have been interchanged from father to son. What a miracle to be able to create something from nothing, just like the Father. The Trinity created a tree in the beginning when there was no tree. We can make amazing things that didn't exist before, too. Creating takes faith. God is near. Everything is a risk, but the Holy Spirit helps us to be inspired. He will prompt us to be partakers in this crazy, wild story of creation. We have plenty of creative genes in us as image-bearers. "We must remember," Justina adds, "not everyone is an artist, which is someone that has devoted their life to a craft. But everyone is creative. I watch so many people shut down when I ask them to be creative because they assume I've asked them to morph into an artist in five minutes. When really all I'm asking is for them to tap into their human right to think for themselves and generate an idea."

Everyone will have low lows when choosing to enter into the creative process. It happens to the best of us, but we don't have to stay there. "Sometimes I will draw or paint something and when I see the result I feel like a fraud," admits Justina matter-of-factly. "I cry out to God. I ask for help, and He helps me. I've given my life to visual art and craft, but that doesn't exclude me from needing the voice of my Father to keep me centered in my work, and needing friends who can speak into my process. It is in this rhythm of submitting to God and humbling myself that the most important thing becomes recreated: my heart."

The enemy hates those who create. He kills, steals and destroys (John 10:10). But the Lord is the Greater One. He is on our side when we try to create; He transforms the ugly parts of us into something beautiful. He is not afraid of those shadow-lands in our lives. If we are frightened of stepping out in childlike faith and making a craft, we can remember Justina, not in a rush. The pressure is off.

Are you feeling the pressure to produce? Pause and take a deep breath. Remember that the Father loves creating with you. He is not demanding your performance, but instead is eagerly waiting to reveal Himself to you in the practical process of what you create with your hands.

BUILDING
A FIRE

BY MELISSA HELSER
INK DRAWING BY KEN HELSER

In the beautiful noise of my everyday, I am learning to listen. In the beautiful schedule of my everyday, I am learning to be flexible. In the beautiful, mundane normal, I am learning to see extravagance in simple moments.

I love winter. I love the invitation it gives. My children notice that our family time grows and deepens in winter months. It gets darker earlier. We stop working sooner. We linger at the dinner table longer. We become slower in a fantastic way. We make fires and sit in the warmth of their presence.

Why is a fire so magical, so inviting? When the fireplace is full of flame and generously giving warmth, it casts a spell over our home. It woos the heart to breathe deeper. It calls to the soul to stop and sit and be still. I am learning to be present in these moments, to give in. My son asked me today if he could start a fire. It was 65 degrees outside, not quite cold enough for a raging fire. He was persistent and kept insinuating how cold he was. I told him that I didn't know if he was old enough to build a fire, and he proudly said, "I am, Dad taught me. He even taught me how to cut kindling and use his hatchet." I suddenly realized it had nothing to do with the fire and everything to do with his desire to show me how grown up he is. I smiled and relinquished the thought of sweating while doing homeschool. "Okay, you can build one." He was pumped.

I went through my normal mom advice: "Be careful."

"I will be, Mom."

"If you play around with a hatchet you can cut your hand off..."

"I know, Mom," he assured me.

The door shut. Thirty minutes later he came in with four pieces of wood. It took him forever, but he was so proud. He proceeded to carefully build a fire in our wood stove just like Jonathan had taught him. I kept asking if he needed help, and he kept assuring me not to worry; he knew exactly what he was doing. He finally had it lit and didn't even use the fire starter sticks that I always use. "Mom, come and see. Look! I did it." It was glorious—the fire and the look on his face. We just sat and stared at it. After a few minutes, he began to doubt that it would keep burning. I could hear the tone of the perfectionist coming out in his self-criticism. "I don't think I did it right. I should have used the starters. I am not good at this." I was astounded by how quickly the overwhelming fear of failure rushed in the room. I am learning to see it quicker and, as a mother, champion the beauty of my kids' hearts. "Cadence, this fire is amazing—you did a great job! I think we should leave it, shut the doors of the wood stove and let it do its magic." We sat down at the kitchen table and began school again. Distracted by our lesson, he forgot about the fire. Until Jonathan walked in the door. "Who made that fire?" We both turned and looked—it was roaring. A glorious smile swept over his face.

His father's approval sealed the deal.

I hope and pray that I continue to have the sensitivity to the Holy Spirit to know when these moments are happening all around me and inviting me to come and feast at the table. Even as I write, I am overcome with emotion that my son is almost thirteen and life is moving like a rushing river that won't be stopped. If I want to experience it, I have to get in it. I have to leave behind all my have-to's and should-have's and what-if's and just give in. My kids invite me into these moments without even knowing it. It is what I love the most about them. I love that all his fear of failure, even in a simple moment, was swallowed up in his father's approval. I pray in this moment that the seemingly insignificant moments of your life that have made you feel like a failure will be gloriously interrupted with the Father's smile. That you would feel the Father of fathers walk into your heart and honor the places you are truly desiring to grow and mature. That His smile would be that warmth, covering you and surrounding you with a beautiful "Well done."

WINTER

POEM BY ROSEMARY GINGERICH
PHOTO BY KEN HELSER

In spring I know your joy and laughter.
In summer I know your abundant love.
In fall I know your smile overflowing into colors,
But in winter, I know your faithfulness, God.
I shed what is only temporary
And my truest self comes forth, bare before You
I stand in all my weakness and frailty.
And yet, You remain.
You never let go of me, never.
Yes, winter sings of your faithfulness,
Declares your faithfulness
To my rawest self. You sow yourself
And stand with me. You never leave, never.
Yes, there is no season more fruitful than winter,
For here I fall into the depths of God
And discover I am cradled by a faithfulness
That never stops giving.
What a privilege to know You in winter, God.

WHAT BLOOMS IN WINTER

{ RECIPE FOR HOPE }

A few years ago, I set out on a journey to discover my favorite flower. What I didn't understand at the time was how seemingly impossible this task would be. As it turns out, I am a lover of flowers. Instead of discovering my favorite one, I've developed a fondness for many varieties of them. I admire poppies for the way they are simultaneously vibrant and delicate. I marvel at the layers of peonies and giggle at the whimsy of snapdragons. Recently though, a friend told me about a flowering bush that is particularly special: camellia.

Camellias are evergreen shrubs notorious for their glossy leaves and full, colorful flowers. These slow-growing bushes have their origins in Asia but are also commonly found in the southern regions of the United States. Like many other flowers, the camellia blooms are robust and vibrant in color. However, what sets these flowers apart is the time of year in which they bloom. Unlike their similar counterparts, camellias come alive between September and May and frequently flower during the winter.

The idea of a bush that flowers in the winter sparked my curiosity. Is it possible that something beautiful could come alive in the winter?

My heart has seen some pretty dismal winter seasons. There was a time in my life where it seemed like my spring and summer seasons began to shrink and my winters became extended. During my final year of high school, my mother was diagnosed with Stage IV breast cancer. She was declared in and out of remission multiple times over the span of four years until she passed away during my final year at University in 2011. Suddenly, this one very intense tragedy took me out, and I was certain that I would always be trapped in this bone-chilling place. I thought I would never recover from this wintry blizzard that had buried my heart.

"We plant this hope in our beautiful seasons by remembering what the Father is doing, by being aware and stewarding thankfulness in our hearts for how He is working in our lives. If we wait until our darkest season to plant hope, it will not grow."

When I think back to this time, my harshest winter, I am surprised by what I find there. Somehow, against the dreary backdrop of my heart, I see how hope bloomed like the camellias. It didn't make sense, and at times, it even offended me. I felt entitled to my anger and hopelessness because of the desolate reality of my circumstances. But it bloomed all the same. I realize now that this hope bloomed because it is what I had cultivated in easier seasons. Just like the camellias, hope must be planted in spring or autumn when the conditions of our hearts seem more favorable. We plant this hope in our beautiful seasons by remembering what the Father is doing, by being aware and stewarding thankfulness in our hearts for how He is working in our lives. If we wait until our darkest season to plant hope, it will not grow.

I have seen hope bloom in the other seasons of my heart many times. I've seen hope wake up in my spring seasons of growing, in my summers of freedom and in my autumns of transition. It looks right and beautiful there, and it was a delight to my soul. But I have never encountered a hope more refreshing than winter's hope, because that is the place where I never thought I would see it bloom.

Prompt: Find a quiet place with the Father. Spend some time letting Him settle your heart, and pray this prayer: "Father, thank you for hope and a reminder of spring and life in the winter seasons of my heart. Holy Spirit, I invite you to remind my heart of times that we have planted hope in previous seasons. Show me where hope is blooming in my heart. How can we tend this hope together?" Journal His voice and allow His hope to refresh your heart.

WRITING AND PAINTING BY ALLIE SAMPSON

YOU'RE FAITHFUL AND I'M THANKFUL

At the turn of late autumn many years ago, I found myself living in a city, constantly surrounded by people on all sides. Regardless of how many people I surrounded myself with, in my heart I was very alone. I tried to mask hurt and heart woundings with busyness, thinking that if I didn't slow down, the brokenness in my life would not be able to catch up with me. In that season, I climbed onto the hamster wheel of performance. This wheel, from the inside, looks like you're going somewhere because you're expending great energy. However, from an outside perspective, it's easy to see that it's a path that goes nowhere, and the energy that was being spent was nothing greater than busywork to fill my days. The spinning wheel was running my life, and I wasn't able to stop it in my own power.

What happened next is nothing short of miraculous. The Lord revealed His undying faithfulness to me and opened a door for me to not only move from where I was living, but also to move from the season in which my life was in. Instead of loneliness, I was invited into family. For the broken places in my heart, the Lord invited me into wholeness, stepping off the wheel of busywork and into His arms that are faithful, steady and true. I was given what I didn't know I needed: family, healing and wholeness.

One of the greatest mysteries is the reality that God knows what we need far greater than we know ourselves. As seasons change, as time passes and I grow, I stand back and evaluate my life. I'll be in the farm kitchen cooking a meal. Or in the garden pulling weeds or harvesting that season's crop. It has happened while walking a trail deep in the woods, amazed by the color of the fall leaves or the blue sky that seems to meld with the tall growing oaks. It's the moment when you think about your life and stand in amazement that the particular moment you are in, is in fact very real. In these moments, I know that the Father is much more present and working in my life than I realize. This, I believe with my whole heart, is a tangible manifestation of the faithfulness and the goodness of God.

In the season of busyness, I was not capable of telling anyone my need because I didn't know what I needed. I knew that I wasn't okay, but I didn't know how to change my situation. I didn't know how to climb off the hamster wheel. The Lord knew that I needed a drastic change, and I made a powerful decision to trust Him. He handed me an invitation to live a whole life, and I accepted.

My challenge to you is a simple one: ask the Father to illuminate where He has consistently been faithful in your life. Where has He brought healing in your life and wholeness to your heart? Where has He met your greatest need? Write a prayer of thanksgiving to the Lord. Let thanksgiving well up in your heart, for you once were lost, but now you're found. You were once blind, but now your eyes have been opened to clearly see.

WRITTEN BY MARTHA MCRAE

TINY HOUSE

POEM BY JESSIE MILLER
DRAWING BY JUSTINA STEVENS

Some people work all their lives
To live somewhere too large.

They tire their hands,
They tire their hearts,
They miss out on the gifts
Only time can give.

Me, I prefer my home tiny.

In my tiny house, I worry less,
Things once lost stay found.

In my tiny house, I am close to You,
Your presence all around.

In my tiny house, every corner fills
With love and understanding.

In my tiny house,
I feel most like myself
I lay my head down and smile.

In my tiny house,
I've found true love and I know
I'll stay here more than a long while.

Living tiny is living full,
Every inch is to be savored.
Living tiny is living full,
Everything is filled with favor.

Living tiny in the home of Love,
Boundaries feel so wide.
Living tiny in the home of You,
I am so happy to abide.

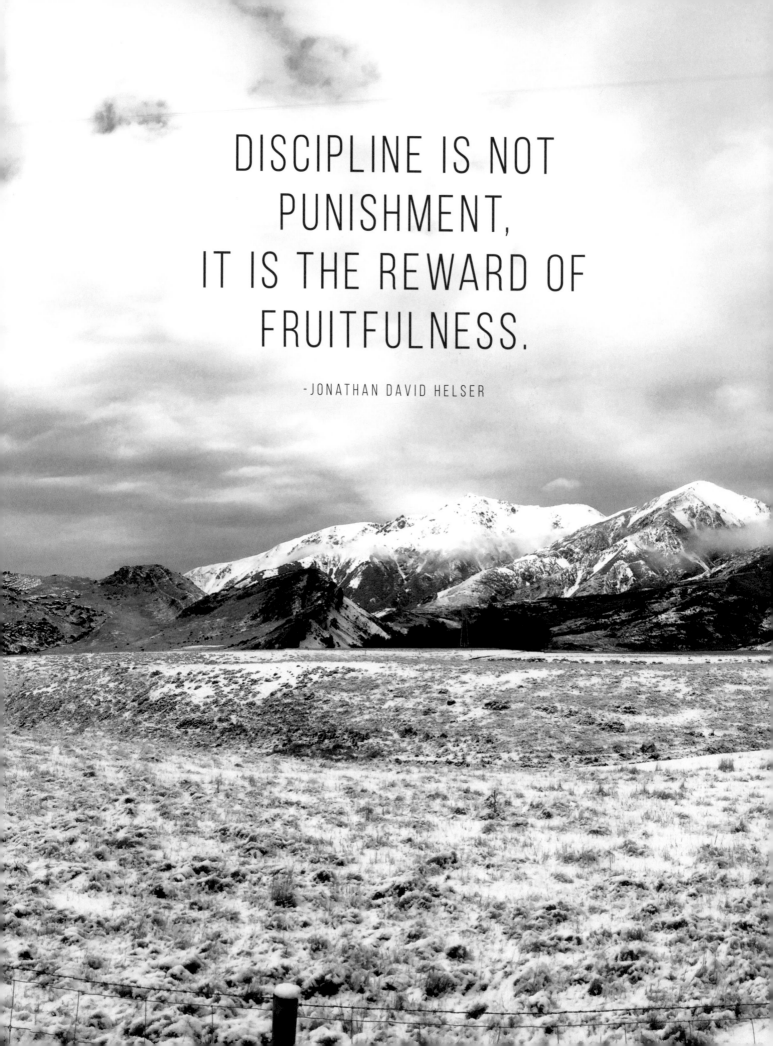

DISCIPLINE IS NOT
PUNISHMENT,
IT IS THE REWARD OF
FRUITFULNESS.

-JONATHAN DAVID HELSER

A COLLECTIVE WRITING
CENTERED AROUND HEARING GOD
IN THE SIMPLE AND ORDINARY THINGS OF LIFE

everything and anything

WRITTEN BY LINDSAY ARMISTEAD, MOLLY SKAGGS
JD GRAVITT, ALLIE SAMPSON & LUKE SKAGGS

ILLUSTRATIONS BY LINDSAY ARMISTEAD

God is waiting for you. He has written your name and address on today's invitation and is ready to encounter you in the simplicity of your daily rhythms. He has planned on meeting you in the quiet of your morning. When the sleep still feels thick in the air, He has come to catch you before you catch hold of all that today brings. Will you let His intention hold you here?

His is the smile beckoning your lips into an upward curve, that first rush of life that tells you your heart is beating and your blood flowing freely. *It is good that you are alive.*

He has already planned into breakfast and coffee, hiding Himself inside the fragrance of the beans, the sound of the tea kettle whistle, the first sip, the deep exhale. He is inviting you to trade in the cynicism you feel towards this repetitive, inglorious routine and instead get lost in the sea of "God is with me".

Glory. He found you. You found Him. Will you press further in?

Your normal for His sacred.
Your inconsistency for His steady pace.
Your cynicism for His faith.
Your self-protection for His defense.
Your surrender for His victorious freedom.
Your unfounded beliefs for the secrets of His heart.

Will you press in? Will you find Him here?
He is waiting for you. Will you come?

MOKA

Reflection by Molly Skaggs

POUR OVER

Reflection by JD Gravitt

Making a lovely cup of coffee using a stovetop espresso maker requires just the right amount of heat and pressure to extract a bold, rich flavor. I have discovered that this has been much like my relationship with the Father in certain seasons of my life; receiving the good gifts He has for me has, at times, looked like I was giving in to an uncomfortable process of yielding to the heat and trusting in the pressure. Yet the beauty of it all is that His love has forever removed the scalding singe in the heat and the crippling fear I used to feel in pressure. Rather, the heat and pressure became the helping hands that worked alongside Him to form goodness from deep within and to bring it out of me. What I am left holding in my heart afterward tastes a lot like the cup of stovetop espresso coffee in my hands; the beauty He fashioned within me has a strong, satisfying flavor meant for deep enjoyment and worth His passionate, patient love.

The thirsty coffee grounds sit expectantly in their freshly ground aroma. I love the artistry of pouring a stream of water over them and watching as they swell and expand, absorbing the water and growing into a beautiful bloom. Water and heat bring the coffee grounds to life, and the result is a delicious and rich dark liquid. I believe the Lord enjoys watching us come to life as well. He patiently and diligently takes time to care for the smallest details of our lives. He gently works in the midst of our process and savors every aroma and flavor released from our hearts. He must love watching us respond to Him, blooming to life. When we're finished brewing, He sits in satisfaction, holding the beautiful fragrance of our lives in His hands.

DRIP

Reflection by Allie Sampson

Most methods of preparing coffee are intended for only one person, but drip coffee has the capacity to serve a group. It is community-style brewing, and it brings people together to share and enjoy. When I prepare a pot of coffee, I get excited as I anticipate giving away hot coffee to friends as they come inside and try to warm up from braving the chilly weather. I know that the fruit of my effort will go beyond myself and will serve the people around me. How many times did Jesus do this in a given day? Jesus said that He came not to be served but to serve (Matthew 20:28), and I believe that this overflowed into His daily life. The next time someone offers you a cup of coffee, close your eyes, breathe in the aroma. Look into the eyes of the person who offered it to you and see the Love that has been pursuing you your whole life. Look into the cup of drip coffee and find Jesus there.

FRENCH PRESS

Reflection by Luke Skaggs

I've used a French press to make coffee for years, but it wasn't until recently that I discovered something vital to the process. Once the coffee is prepared, you must pour it into a separate container, away from the grounds, so that the coffee ceases cooking and won't become bitter to the taste. I see this as a picture of our lives with the Father. He loves to pour gifts from His heart into us. He is not in a hurry with our process, but He patiently waits until what He poured in has beautifully changed us. I've had the privilege to learn, through living in community, that the taste of my life is best, not when I stay hidden inside of myself, but when I allow the gift of Jesus inside of me to be poured out and shared with others. He prepares us with such detail and care, and at the end of the day, I believe His heart for us is to know what a fine cup we are to Him and to the world around us.

EVERY SMALL DETAIL

PROMPT BY LINDSAY ARMISTEAD

"The earth is the Lord's and the fullness thereof" (Psalm 24:1, ESV).

Ken Helser, a father of this land, has poured a foundational truth into our hearts with this saying: "You can find God in everything and miss Him in anything. In everything, God has a voice."

God has hidden Himself in every small detail of your life. Yes, His longing for us is so deep, God has even hidden Himself inside the simplicity of the way you make your morning coffee. In everything, He is speaking.

"It is the glory of God to conceal things, but the glory of kings is to search things out" (Proverbs 25:2, ESV).

Choose a simple process that you engage in everyday. Begin by thanking the Lord for this process. Then ask the Lord to open your eyes to see the way He has hidden Himself inside this simple part of your life. It is our privilege to search God out! Celebrate the way God has pursued you in this process and respond to His nature overflowing into every area of your life.

HOLES

POEM BY PHYLLIS UNKEFER
PHOTO BY KEN HELSER

I want to dig holes everywhere.
Under trees. On hilltops. In the middle of fields.
I want to dig holes
Where tall grass kneels to the wind.
Along road-ties, where ants journey in shining black streams.

I want to dig beside the creek,
Under the cursive of dragonflies gliding.
In the forest, where leaves braid a cathedral, glowing and green.

I want to dig holes for you to step quietly in.
You'll take off your shoes,
Hold your skirt,
And let your feet touch down, Soft.

Then, if you don't mind, I'll come looking for you.
I'll wander with open eyes
Till I come around some bend, or down some hill,
And I find you, Planted.

Wherever you go, my friend, you have a place.
Space to spread your roots.
To feel how gladly water defies gravity and seeps up through you.
To see how gracefully you were made to bend and lean,
and dance with Daylight.

One day, I'll peer past the flowers to see you: Slender and swaying.
Ankle deep and arms raised, you are full of the warmth of being.
And I see your thoughts.
They turn into seeds that spill from your hands.
Your dreams give little mind to where they land
Only knowing that they know all they need to know to grow.

My friend, did you know
There is One who came before?
At the start of all things,
He was the first to dig holes.
He carved out enough space.
Now, wherever you go, you have a place
Where all the seeds of who you are can land.
Take root. Expand.
For they know all they need to know
To grow.

SNOWED IN

WRITTEN BY JOEL CASE PHOTO BY KEN HELSER

I have consistent memories through my childhood of my dad waking up early when it had snowed to snow-blow the driveway, shovel and salt the steps and clear a pathway to the door. When the roads were bad enough, school would be called off on the news, and my dad wouldn't have to go to work. Those were glorious days!

Being snowed in was awesome. It meant we were gifted with permission to spend extra time with our families. There was no work and no school—just rest and play—outside in the wonderland, together by a warm fire, drinking hot cocoa and playing board games. We were closed in to remember what rest and family are all about, and maybe in a time when we didn't realize how much we needed it. These days were opportunities to reset how you did life, when the roads were clear and schools and work were open, a reminder of what is essential.

Sometimes it takes God snowing us in for our hearts to enter home again. Often we forget His nature and get lost in all sorts of other ways of living. We need His rest. God's snow days are the times when the "shoulds" and "coulds" that plague us are silenced by a thick blanket of white from the heavens. It's a resting that comes upon us, and it is God's doing. Works cease. The Father of fathers steps in with His kindness and rescues us, giving us permission to rest.

"He restores my soul" (Psalm 23:3, ESV).

The beautiful truth is that the rest God shows us in those times is always available to us. The rest that we experience in those times is a rest that Scripture exhorts us to work to enter into during the other days and seasons of the year. We can live at rest and at home; we can choose it and work at it. This is part of our inheritance as children of God.

Remember | Sit down with your journal and survey moments in your life when God snowed you in and gave you rest, when He came like snow, and pressed you into home. What was it like? Journal about that time.

Consider | Have you fully received that rest? Are you working to enter and live from that place daily? Or have you let go of the beauty of who God showed you He is? It's time again to recover that rest. It was God's gift to you to keep.

Commit | Read John 14:26. Make a commitment in your heart to the Lord to walk out the rest He gave to your soul. Ask Holy Spirit to remind you of any way you have let go of that hope and to help you recover it again.

Bark

WRITTEN BY MELISSA HELSER
PHOTOGRAPHY BY JONATHAN & MELISSA HELSER

I believe in the power of stillness. The beauty of the quiet, rejuvenating our souls and reminding us of the reality of our smallness and the Master's bigness. I am a lover of the woods, and I have tipped my hat to the mighty giants of the forest. The tall ones that tower over our fear and insecurity. The ones that root deep and reach high and wait. Wait for fullness. I have run my hands along their outer shell, their covering. The bark that protects their life. I have walked for hours and admired how each one has given into the growing. The growing that requires dying. If it refused to die, it would refuse to live. Their sheath that appears rigid and broken comes from their layer of life flowing up and down. And as it grows and expands, it gives in to the process and dies and transforms into an armor of beauty.

The giants wear their armor not to hide in fear but to protect what is really there.

They cover and clothe themselves in a hard shell of their story. "I was this big…but I rooted deep and drank Heaven, and I grew. My clothes cracked and tore but became stronger in the expansion of my confidence. My layers of life keep living as I keep digging. They grow and are full of newness and then they die and become my shield and my strength. They keep out the cold and wind and all those things that seek to eat away at my life's works…growth. I am not afraid of my seasons. My seasons bring about my heart; my seasons keep telling my story over and over again. And if you could see my heart, you would see all the moments surrounding it that I gave in."

Seasons sometimes clothe us with frayed, torn opinions. Ones birthed out of cynicism and stale judgments. Aren't you tired of feeling dressed in words and thoughts that have been birthed out of death and not life, out of sorrow and not hope? When we wake up and put on a covering of truth and beauty, when we open our eyes and choose life, we choose to tell all the dead things birthing dead things to keep their rags. We will be clothed in something that is real, something that comes from life and therefore protects life and creates life. We don't have to be a product of hopelessness. Can we find the courage to tell it that its death is not part of our story, not part of our norm? Our death to fear, insecurity, pride brings us closer to life. Closer to truth. When we give in to life, it creates am armor of truth around our souls. It protects us from the wind and the rain of doubt and the pests that seek to eat away our belonging. We will learn to give in and love our cracked, torn stories. Don't despise your bark, the layers that have been made out of joy or hardship; even our suffering bears life, and not all armor is bad, if it is armor to protect that which matters the most—our beautiful heart.

When He showed them the scars in His hands and His side, He invited us into His cracked, scarred covering. He invited us into His pain and His victory. And He inspired us to be unashamed of the seasons that feel like they have left scars on our hearts. Those scars are the things that give us strength, give us hope. Wear your covering with confidence. Know it is unique and beautiful and shows every moment you gave in to the process of growth. Oh that we would grow deep and tall. That we would allow the armor of a life to protect our hearts and become the giants that the broken and tired world can walk up to and run their hands over our stories and feel and see our brokenness and our victory. I tip my hat to the giants of the forest—once again they have taught me a great truth. I am thankful I had the eyes to see it and the heart to hear it. May we never stop seeing the Kingdom hidden in the world around us. Those who are alive will always hear the whisper in the most unlikely places.

SEASONS PAST

{ RECIPE FOR GOD'S VERSION OF SUCCESS }

Do you ever compare the season your heart is in now to the seasons past? Do you find yourself thinking back to a season where you felt more "together" than you do right now? Perhaps there was a time in your life when you felt like the Lord spoke to you more, or at least you listened better. Maybe your quiet time has changed its form, or your role in a community has shifted and it has left you with a feeling of guilt or shame. This guilt says that there was a time when you were able to give the Lord what He wanted, and that is no longer the case. We label ourselves as failures and falsely believe that the Lord agrees. We as humans have a desire to classify everything based on what we "know." When something new arises, we want to connect it to things we have experienced in some way before. I believe this desire goes back to the Garden. God said, "Do not eat from the tree of the knowledge of good and evil" (Genesis 2:17). He knew it would be too much for us. But we did it anyway, and now we try to classify everything we experience as one or the other—good or evil, success or failure. Our perspective is so small. We can't see the bigger picture, the "all things working together." So we filter life experiences based on what feels right or wrong, what worked or what didn't. We judge based on the little we know. I believe we often distance ourselves from the Lord because we see Him as we see ourselves: a critic, judging our current performance compared to our last season's performances. When we are succeeding, He is happy and things feel good, and when we are failing, He is not happy, and things feel bad. We bite the fruit of knowledge over and over again instead of eating from the Tree of Life.

"Success is not a formula with concrete feelings attached to it. Success is trust in the One who knows your story better than you."

I want to encourage you to lay down your need to feel certain you are succeeding as it relates to what felt right in the past. Life with Jesus is all encompassing, and we are moving from glory to glory. Please, lay down the ruler of success that you brought with you from last season. It will not measure correctly in your new one. Success is not a formula with concrete feelings attached to it. Success is trust in the One who knows your story better than you. God does not need you to prove you are becoming better than you were. Growth with Him is life with Him. It is cyclical, not linear. He is growing different parts of you at different times. Growth in the Kingdom is not like height tally marks on a wall. God is not making sure your one mark keeps getting higher. He is not comparing you to your brothers and sisters. He is not crossing His fingers for a growth spurt. He is present, loving you in this very moment. He is tending to the garden of your heart. He is caring for you more than you can comprehend. Lay down the ruler of seasons past. Only He knows what success looks like for you in this season, and I believe it is different than what you think.

Prompt: Pray this prayer: "Father, forgive me for seeing you as the critic of my heart. Forgive me for comparing my past performance with my present. I confess that you are not a God who demands performance from me. Holy Spirit, show me what growth looks like for me right now."

BY JESSIE MILLER / PHOTO BY MELISSA HELSER

Learning the Woods

WRITTEN BY LINDSAY ARMISTEAD
PAINTING BY JESSIE MILLER

A Place for the Heart sits on a beautiful piece of wooded land just outside the heart of North Carolina, and those who have been privileged to live here for a season know these woods well. Our Sophian woods are sculpted of families of giant oak trees. Poplars shoot straight as arrows into the sky. Spindly dogwoods stand thick at the edge of the forest, and grapevine sprawls low across the crunchy, wooded floor, evidence of our nearby Muscadine vine that has been a late summer's meal for many birds.

There is a creek that winds around the outskirts of our land, hemming us in on three sides. And just beyond the boundary lines are full, rolling hills, the feet of the ancient Uwharrie mountain range that have been laid low over time. My first summer on the farm, I was invited on a guided tour of the woods by one of Sophia's native adventurers, David Shaver. We began on a trail at the back of our property but quickly fell off any resemblance of a path, and I was suddenly at the mercy of David's ability to navigate us through these unfamiliar timberlands. Luckily, David knew the secrets of these Sophian woods. After all, he didn't need to follow the paths he had carved with his own axe and loppers. Two years and many wooded walks later, I have only just begun to uncover the truths that my friend David has been reveling in for seasons: learning the nature of the woods.

This past June, I braved a journey through the woods from an unfamiliar trailhead. Unlike the paths I had so often walked, this trail was enveloped by scaffolds of pine trees, and their needles softened the ground under my feet. What began as a confident adventure soon turned into a mild question: "Where am I?" Then the question deepened into doubt: "I don't know where I am."

I laugh now at the absurd thoughts I had in my half hour of being lost—those wild thoughts, the outrageous but overpowering notions of fear and defeat. "What if I can't backtrack my way out of the woods? What if my sense of direction is totally off? What if I never make it home?"

It was in that moment that my faithful guide, the Holy Spirit, spoke to me with a new thought. "Lindsay, you know these woods. You know these woods." I had given so many quiet mornings, so many silent evenings, to learning these woods. I may not have known exactly where I was, but I knew exactly where I was. My questions of panic were swallowed up by His steady questions of empowerment. "What are these woods like? What have you learned about their nature? Remember the secrets they told you." No longer was I caught up in the fear of losing myself. I was caught up in the joy of Him finding me here. That is exactly like my Jesus would do it.

In a morning of brief distress, the Lord painted a picture of His love for me. Sometimes we may not know exactly where we are. Seasons change; well-worn paths get swallowed up in a sea of color and then disappear. The steps we once took are blanketed by a white season that is bringing change to everything. These winter woods will look nothing like they did in the glory of summer.

The seasons change, but His nature does not change. The Lord reforms the same questions He once asked me, stirring up faith in my heart. "What am I like, Lindsay? What have you learned about my nature? Remember the secrets I told you." And all of a sudden I know exactly where I am. I look up into the towering boughs of His faithfulness and mercy. I'm standing in the ever-sprawling vine of His love. A stream of peace hems me in behind and before. I drink deeply of His steadfast nature and take the hand of my Friend as we set out to carve a new path, the beautiful evidence of my journey with Him.

Sing Winter

WRITTEN BY JONATHAN DAVID HELSER

PHOTO BY JOEL CASE

One Christmas, Melissa and I decided to surprise our son, Cadence, with a ukulele. A couple of days before that Christmas, we had planned to stay up late on a Friday night after the kids had fallen asleep to bake cookies and wrap their gifts. As the house was filling with the aroma of Melissa's baking, I was walking around the kitchen trying to play Christmas songs on Cadence's new ukulele. I was doing my best trying to sing the old duet "Baby It's Cold Outside," and Melissa was singing back to me as she put cookies in the oven. The last thing I was expecting to happen that night was to write a new song, especially on the instrument I was supposed to be wrapping, but suddenly in a very ordinary moment of life, something extraordinary started to fall upon us.

While stumbling through the chords of the old song, I began to feel the melody of a new song descending. I started singing lyrics around the theme of Winter singing her song to me through the silence of the snowflakes. I don't know if it was the flour on Melissa's apron or the anointing from the cookies she was baking, but she started singing a response to my lyrics as if she had become Winter herself singing back to me. Melissa caught eyes with me, and we both knew what was happening: a new song was being born. As songwriters you wait for moments of inspiration to come, but you can never make them happen. You long for these moments like children in winter with their sleds in hand, waiting on the clouds to provide them the substance that turns their normal world into something magical. Melissa and I spent the rest of that evening riding that moment of inspiration and writing our first song about winter. When we woke up that next overcast and sleepy Saturday morning, there were no presents wrapped, but we had a new song that was almost finished. After breakfast the kids settled down to watch a Christmas movie, and Melissa and I slipped into our bedroom to try and finish writing the song without Cadence hearing us playing his ukulele. As we were finishing the last verse, we were interrupted by the joyful squeals of our two children playing outside. We looked out our window and were astonished to see them playing in a surprise snowstorm. None of the weather reports had mentioned the slightest chance of snow. It rarely snows where we live, so anytime it falls our whole world stands still for as long as it's on the ground. We could hardly believe that the snow started falling as we finished the last verse of the song. Our normal Saturday morning had been overtaken by the beauty and majesty of winter.

Hear the snowflakes falling
Winter's calling my name
The silent song she's singing
What's she trying to say?
Can I fall like glory to wash your year away?
All that remains was really meant to stay
Come and clothe me Winter, I really need a change
With silent redemption, Cover me with grace
Hear the song of beauty, Melodies and sounds
Cover you in white love.
The joy you lost but now have found
Sing, sing Winter. Sing me your silent song.

Redemption came like the silent snow that falls while we sleep—the kind where you wake up and the entire landscape has changed. The dark and barren colors of the cold world, are transformed to bright white glory that almost blinds you when you look out the window to see a brand new world. The snowflakes echo the silent redemption plan of a King who came as a baby and became the Savior, who stood silent as a lamb before the shearer. His silent sacrifice covered the whole earth in redemption that turned crimson stains as white as snow.

THERE IS NO DIVIDE

POEM BY KATELAND HILTY

You are my steadfast, You never change.
Not land, seas or heavens
could keep You from me.

There is no divide.

You are always by my side,
Pursuing me out of my fears,
You always draw near.

There is no lover that does what You do,
Your love seeps into my veins
and I begin to love like You.

Love, never stop coming toward me,
Love, never stop changing me,
Love, let there be no divide.

WINTRY MIX OF OUR FATHER

{ RECIPE FOR SEEING GOD'S FAITHFULNESS }

During the winter of my first year of college, my little hometown in middle Tennessee saw one of its craziest snowfalls. I remember showing up for class only to be told that I would be heading straight back home. The temperatures had plummeted about twenty degrees, and wet snow and ice began to pile up on highways and car windshields. My normal commute turned into a messy, white nightmare within half-an-hour. At the time, I did not have much practice driving in those kinds of conditions, but, thank goodness, my dad was on his way to get me. Our drive home was madness! We literally inched our way back to our house while watching cars slide like hockey pucks across the other traffic lanes and into ditches. I was feeling pretty relieved that I was not the one in the driver's seat. My dad was the old pro who had seen snows much worse than this in the eastern Kentucky mountains where he grew up. He did not seem afraid at all. He was completely calm and knew exactly what to do. There was something about that particular snow day that sparked a glorious spontaneity inside of my dad's heart. As soon as we got home, he went into his bedroom to change into his favorite flannel pajamas. He then started up a beautiful roaring fire in the living room fireplace. After disappearing down to the basement, he quickly emerged with packages of frozen venison in his hands. "Oh boy," he cheered, "I can make that deer meat chili I've been wanting to try. And what a perfect day for it, too!" I watched him whiz around the kitchen with a sparkling delight. This was my daddy in a winter season's suddenly inclement moment: joyful, warm and at rest. Here was a man who just rescued me from a treacherous wintry circumstance, now fully enjoying it and creating magic in its midst. I now understand I might never have seen that side of him if that snow had not sent our world into a wild spin that morning.

"The world's a huge stockpile of God-wonders and God-thoughts. Nothing and no one comes close to you! I start talking about you, telling what I know, and quickly run out of words. Neither numbers nor words account for you".
Psalm 40:5, MSG

Winter comes to us and brings with her a mixed bag full of surprises. Yet we can be thankful for these seasons of our hearts because they only prove the consistency and fidelity of the Father's nature all the more to us. Though there may be moments of uncertainty and fear, He is capable of creating spontaneous wonder and delight within them. His peaceful heart enables our hearts to be at peace. His joy ignites joy in us, even when things are scary and hard. He is always at rest, able to take on any kind of circumstance with a sparkle in His eye saying, "Now, let's have some fun, shall we?" What a brilliant, wonderful Father He is!

Prompt: Find a warm, quiet space with the Father and open up a conversation with Him like this: "Father, thank you for this season I am in right now. In the scary as well as the beautiful, you long for me to know you better. Which parts of your nature are you uncovering for me in this season?" Journal His response to you and enjoy this moment of reflection with Him.

BY MOLLY KATE SKAGGS

WE HAVE THIS HOPE

{ RECIPE FOR GOD'S VERSION OF SUCCESS }

When it takes too much effort to hope, or when hope disappoints me, I know I have put my hope in the wrong place. It is so easy to begin to hope in circumstances. "If only this would happen, or if only that was gone, then life would be so good!" There is no hope there. Circumstances constantly change. Circumstances are not true indicators for a promise fulfilled or a victory given. I have to take my eyes off of the seen and put them on the unseen! My hope is in Jesus. My faith is in Him. He is so good and faithful. He will bring our circumstances in line with His promise—that is our hope.

Hope is an amazing gift from the Lord. Hope sustains me, centers me, inspires me and delights me. And often, hope rescues me. I love seeing hope as an anchor; solid, rough and heavy, something I can wrap my hands around and feel. There have been times in my life when all I can do is hold on to hope. I grab hold and I don't let go. Hope becomes solid and real inside of me, keeping me in the heart of Jesus. Hope becomes faith. In the darkest hours when prayers can't be formed, I hope in Him and know that He is there in the most holy place interceding for me.

"We have this hope as an anchor for the soul, firm and secure."
Hebrews 6:19, NIV

"With joy you will draw water from the wells of salvation" (Isaiah 12:3, NIV). I often draw up a bucket full of hope. Hope implies a longing, a desire for what we don't yet have. Hope keeps me seeking the heart of God, dreaming for the future and staying excited about life. If I become cynical or resentful, that is a good indicator that I am losing hope for my life. Fresh vision from the Lord fills me with hope, and hope courses through my veins carrying away any spiritual hardening of the arteries. Hope is in Jesus.

Prompt: Pray this prayer: "Father, thank you for the hope you give. Thank you for filling my life with hope and promise. I live with joy in the present and I eagerly look forward to what you have waiting around the bend. Forgive me when I put my hope in the wrong place, in either a person or circumstance. Let my hope be anchored in you. Holy Spirit illuminate my heart and show me the vision of a life filled with hope and walked out in promise." Journal your thoughts and His response to you.

BY KAYE SHAVER

ASKING FOR HELP

PROMPT BY JOEL CASE
PHOTO BY SYDNEE MELA

"I have chosen you and not cast you off; fear not, for I am with you; be not dismayed, for I am your God; I will strengthen you, I will help you, I will uphold you with my righteous right hand" (Isaiah 41:9-10, ESV).

What weighs heavy on your soul? Are you tired inside? Do you know that Jesus has a restful way that He wants to teach you? He wants all your fear, anxiety, pressure, regret, hopelessness and judgement. He has already taken them, in His body, on the cross. He went the distance in love for you before you first opened your eyes and entered this world. This is a true reality for you to feast on and be impacted by.

Write down and name what is heavy on your heart today. Now, full of faith, trust that Jesus is near you and tell Him about it. Ask Him for help. Confess your need and that you cannot carry these things on your own. Then wait on the Lord. Let Him attend to your needs by the Holy Spirit. End your time with this prayer: "Jesus, I recieve this rest. Thank you so much. Teach me how to live in this rest. I believe your promise and hold it in hope and expectation in my heart."

RUST

POEM AND PHOTO
BY JD GRAVITT

Metal has a secret, I was told.
His deep warm surface no longer cold.
Fire escapes the metal sides.
Beauty finds her home where the metal hides.

Metal holds a secret and finds safety in the sheets of beauty
Her fiery warm waves wrap over his heart
The worn metal wears a sheet of strength
The waves of water changing the color of his leaves.
No question of worth, he stands for all eyes to see
The years of rain and snow built his authority.

So what can we say about metal?
This fabrication, fragile as a flower petal.
Do the wares of time ruin what he was made to be?
Or reveal his ancient majesty?

HOLGA

WRITING AND FILM HOLGA PHOTOS
BY JONATHAN HELSER

Today our family is going on an adventure—we are going to explore the Oregon sand dunes. It is an area of windswept sand that is the largest expanse of sand dunes in North America; it is truly a magical place. I am bringing along a Holga camera to remember this day. I have never used a Holga before. A Holga is basically a chunky, toy-like camera made almost entirely of plastic. It's gloriously unpredictable. It has no bells or whistles. The features of this little camera would be considered defects in any other camera, but that's what makes it so fantastic. It is wonderfully unreliable. The one dependable quality of this camera is its imperfect results. As a photographer who loves to shoot with my Cannon 5d Mark II, this piece of plastic cuts right through my dependency on technology. I feel like an amateur, a novice, a child, and there is something so liberating about that. I can feel my perfectionist prison walls crumbling under the weight of this little camera in my hands. My options have been reduced to twelve exposures on a roll of film. This outdated camera is causing me to slow down and carefully choose which moment I want to remember. It's like when you decide to walk instead of driving. You see things you would never have seen in a fast-moving vehicle. In such a fast-paced culture, we can arrive at our destination quicker than ever, but are we seeing all the beauty of the in-between?

Are we moving so fast through this life that we are missing the symphony that is playing all around us? When I sit down and listen to a vinyl record on my old turntable, I always hear depths in the music that I don't hear through my car stereo system. We live in a time where we can hear music in every store or elevator, but are we stopping to hear the glorious refrain? We can take endless amounts of pictures with our phones, but are we slowing down to see beauty in each moment? Find a way to intentionally savor the process. Walk instead of driving. Handwrite the letter instead of e-mailing it. Cook a meal and stay around the table a little longer. Choose to slow down.

LIKE CLAY

I am a potter and this past year I have fallen in love with the potter's wheel. When I'm at the wheel, before I can even think about forming the clay into a beautiful shape, I must focus all of my attention to the centering process. The purpose of this process is to bring all the knots which live deep inside the clay up to the surface so that my hands can smooth them out and the clay's weight is distributed evenly into the center of the wheel. This allows me to successfully make a shape later on without the knots fighting against my hands. It is important when centering, however, to move all of the clay up from deep within and not just the clay on the surface; otherwise, the knots will remain and the clay will not center. Then it cannot be made into a shape without collapsing or deforming.

Often times, I go through seasons where I feel like a ball of clay, full of knots that are coming to the surface. Although my natural tendency is to become overwhelmed, I know that it is the kindness of the Father wrapping His hands around me and moving all of the clay from deep inside me to the surface so He can smooth out my knots and recenter me into His hands. This is how I am shaped into a beautiful vessel.

Prompt: Maybe you are in a season where you see all your knots coming to the surface. Ask the Holy Spirit to show you the deep work that the Father is doing inside of you. Journal His response with the truth in mind that He is a trustworthy, kind and patient Father who desires to make you more whole and complete in Him. Then write a response back to Him, giving Him permission to come in and shape your heart with His loving hands.

WRITTEN BY ROSEMARY GINGERICH

ALL THAT'S LEFT IS EVERGREEN

POEM AND PAINTING BY JUSTINA STEVENS

When Cold settles
And every love note has fallen
I watch morning turn dew to frost
All that's left is evergreen

When slumber feels close
And drowsy light persuades me
As layers of wool wrap me
Feet shuffle on wood

Quiet graces every corner
Where does warmth go?

When I pull down the brittle wreath
And the music ends
And the once white blanket
Is mixed with mud

When gifts are piled
My heart is still and desperate
In my smallest room, silent and honest
Prayer echos against blank walls

No answer
Just movement toward me
A warm hand in mine
I breathe in Cold air

Quiet graces every corner
I rest in this year's snow

THE REAL PROMISED LAND IS WHERE
MY EYES ARE HEALED, AND I CAN
SEE GOD FOR WHO HE REALLY IS:
A FAITHFUL FATHER.

-MELISSA HELSER

THE CAGELESS BIRDS

"We escaped like a bird from a hunter's trap. The trap is broken, and we are free!" Psalm 124:7, NLT

The Cageless Birds is a community of leaders and artisans from Sophia, North Carolina founded by Jonathan and Melissa Helser. We are drawn together by an authentic passion for the Gospel of Jesus and a commitment to live out wholeness in community. We believe in the risk of saying yes to flying out of the cage of fear and soaring on the wings of true identity. We have fallen in love with the rhythm of pouring out our lives in ministry and then refilling our hearts in rhythms of family, friendship and creativity. This is sustainability. This is what it means to fly high and build home.

As leaders, we believe in and are committed to seeing a generation transformed by the Gospel. This commitment is walked out through our discipleship school, The 18 Inch Journey. Here, we set a table for students from around the world to come and encounter the love of the Father, the power of the Cross, the sustainability of the Holy Spirit, and the beautiful transformation that happens in community.

As artisans, we come alive in creating goods throughout the year that help support our growing families and the mission of our schools. Whether it's creating music, writing books or cultivating one of our many other art forms, we are anchored with joy in the pursuit of excellence in all that we do.

For more on the Cageless Birds, visit our website and online store at *cagelessbirds.com.*

Design and Layout
Melissa Helser, Justina Stevens and Lindsay Armistead.

Copy Editors
Sarah Roach and Allie Sampson

"Two Pieces of Dry Land" photo - David Burbach
Hand lettered type - Lindsay Armistead
Cover photo - Jonathan Helser
Pattern prints and "Holga" title - Justina Stevens

[1] *Cultivate definition:"cultivate." Merriam-Webster.com. Merriam-Webster, 2016.*

[2] *Recipe definition: "recipe." Merriam-Webster.com. Merriam-Webster, 2016.*

[3] *Prompt definition: "prompt." Merriam-Webster.com. Merriam-Webster, 2016.*

[4] *Defining Moment definition: "defining moment." Dictionary.com, 2016.*

[5] *Story definition: "story." Dictionary.com, 2016.*

[6] *Poem definition: "poem." Dictionary.com, 2016.*